SENIOR INSTRUCTOR
Chaplain Dale A. Scadron, M.Di

Chaplain Scadron is a graduate c. ...g...... ....
He earned his Master of Divinity and Doctorate in Theology
degrees from Crossroads Bible College
and Theological Seminary as well as a
Doctorate degree in Literature (honoris
causa) from Omega Bible Institute and
Seminary. Chaplain Scadron is an
ordained minister with the International
Church of the Foursquare Gospel, and
holds ecclesiastical endorsement as an institutional
chaplain. Chaplain Scadron is founder and president of
Chaplains International, Inc., and founder and chancellor of
Signet Bible College and Theological Seminary. Chaplain
Scadron served, as a fulltime chaplain with the Kern County
Sheriff Detentions Bureau and was instrumental in the
development of the law enforcement chaplains program.
Chaplain Scadron served five years as divisional chaplain
with the Los Angeles Police Department and eight years as
a chaplain for the Glendale Police Department in Glendale
California. Currently he serves on staff as a chaplain at the
Taft Federal Correctional Facility located in Taft, California.

CHAPLAINCY 101

Published by, Chaplains College Press,

CLASS OUTLINE

Courseware

LESSON 1

Introduction to Industrial Chaplaincy

Institutional Chaplaincy is a ministry that is unique and varied. Institutional chaplains serve correctional facilities, police and fire agencies, medical centers, senior-care, universities and colleges, etc.

Pastor vs Chaplain

Pastors and Chaplains share many tasks and competencies. Both have experienced a special call to ministry and service. Both are teachers, caregivers, witnesses of their own faith, and advocates for people. Both have a desire to equip people to grow in spiritual maturity. So you might ask, what is the difference? Perhaps the greatest difference is the setting in which the ministry is provided. Congregational Pastors usually minister to a group of people who have like or similar religious beliefs and who share many common cultural identities, such as, language, geographic location, socioeconomic status, or ethnic identity. Chaplains, on the other hand, usually minister to a group of people of many different religious beliefs or no religious beliefs at all. These people usually represent many different cultural identities, including those of education, profession, and political persuasion. Community clergy are given authority by a congregation or ecclesiastical body, whereas Chaplains are given authority by the institution that employs them in addition to the ecclesiastical body that endorses them. Chaplains are clergy members from any one of various religious faiths who has chosen to minister to a group of people outside the walls of a church or other house of worship. From a Christian perspective, their role is pastoral, prophetic, and priestly, even while being nonreligious to those who profess no religion. They enter the ministry situation with no personal agenda and the attitude of a servant.

Christian Chaplains are an extension of Christ's ministry to all people. There is a common misconception that Chaplains have left the real ministry to do social ministry. This could not be farther from the truth. Jesus did make a habit of regular synagogue attendance, and be often taught there (Luke 4:16-24). However, most of His ministry was very much outside the walls of the institutional "church." He taught on the seashore, on mountaintops, over dinner tables, and along the roads as He walked.

Additionally, He did not limit His ministry to devout Jews, but befriended sinners and tax collectors, healed Romans and Samaritans.

He preached to crowds of mixed Jewish and Gentile ancestry.

Following Christ's example of cross-cultural ministry, Chaplains provide many forms of caring ministry to countless people in various places beyond the walls of the church. Mathew 25 concerns Jesus' teaching about the value of all persons, not just those who shared His ethnicity, culture and religion. Jesus taught that if people wanted to be considered righteous and "inherit the kingdom" of God, they were to minister to all persons, particularly those considered the "least of these. "Many of the people who were considered the "least of these" are still with us. They are the homeless, the disabled, the uneducated, and the terminally ill. Chaplains are called to minister to the disenfranchised of society, the "least of these." Additionally however, Chaplains face the challenge of providing loving care to all they encounter, even those whose social or economic status does not seem to warrant help or those whose celebrity already commands attention or assistance.

Other times the challenge is providing and demonstrating the love of God to those who do not seem to deserve care, the perpetrator of a heinous crime or the one who threatens the Christian faith. The Mathew text speaks to the Chaplain of the innate worth of all persons, not just those who agree with their religion, share their culture, or look like them. Because we are all "created in the image of God" (Genesis 1:27), we are all entitled to, and worthy of, compassionate ministry and respect.

Chaplains follow Gods example by loving and caring for any person regardless of age, gender, culture, race, color, or ethnic background. Jesus instructed people to take the initiative and go to those in need, not wait for people to come to them, specifically to those who are "sick or in prison." There is certainly biblical precedence for taking ministry to the people rather than waiting for them to come to the minister. The significance of the pattern for going to people in order to minister is that it was common in biblical times, that there is a long-standing precedent for this form of ministry, and that it is not a new or modern delivery system of ministry that should be looked at with suspicion.

The Chaplains mandate is to be involved in the crisis of people's lives, regardless of personal religious convictions; the Chaplain is often in the position of ministering to the basic needs of others. That ministry is not a hook to obligate the client to remain for the sermon or any other overtly religious teaching or service but a genuine example of the Chaplains own living faith. Ministry is provided without conditions and unrealistic expectations, it should be out of genuine love and compassion. The Chaplain must always exercise wisdom in choosing the appropriate ministry intervention for each situation.

Attending to the basic human physiological needs of survival must often take precedence over evangelizing with the gospel message. Starving people perceive that they have a greater need for food than they do for religion, and no amount of religion will assuage their aching bellies.

The cold, the hungry, the thirsty, the hurting-they find little comfort in religious tracts and platitudes. They need blankets and a place of physical and emotional safety. The good works of Chaplains and other ministers often open the doors for faith. Jesus made ministry practical in order to make evangelism possible. James also made this point when he asserted that by our good works (deeds) others would be able to see that our faith is genuine. (James 2:14-17).Another Chaplaincy concept modeled for us in scripture is what Jesus asked for and needed from others during His darkest moments in the Garden of Gethsemane (Mathew 26:36-45). Twice Jesus asked His disciples to "stay and keep watch." No doing for would help Him in that hour. Not even His closest disciples Peter, and John could do anything for Him except to stay and keep watch.

Keeping watch involves active emotional and spiritual presence in addition to physical presence. Jesus was asking for His disciple's presence. He needed His disciples just to stay and be with Him. The Chaplain, as a representative or ambassador of Christ is privileged to stay with someone who is emotional, physical, or in spiritual pain, without trying to fix the person's problems, offer unsolicited advice, or recite religious platitudes. Being present in a time of crisis offers tremendous moral support, the fact that the Chaplain is there may enable them to believe that God has not abandoned them and communicates Gods assurance, "Fear not, for I am with you." (*Isaiah 41:10NKJV*)[i]By (CI) Chaplain Norberto Guzman, B.A., M.C.C. / Signet Bible College and Theological Seminary

Chaplains in Law Enforcement

Law enforcement Chaplains serve municipal law enforcement agencies, such as city police, or county agencies that include sheriff's departments. They also serve state agencies that include rangers, state patrol, and highway patrol. In addition to these entities, there is a broader field in federal agencies that includes the Secret Service, the FBI, and U.S. Border Patrol. In all such settings, Chaplains provide direct services to a particular station or office as well as being available to the rest of the department or agency. Law enforcement Chaplains have many duties that relate directly to officers and staff of the law enforcement agency. For example, they may ride with officers or accompany them on duty when requested; attend roll calls, staff meetings, and other departmental meetings counsel officers, departmental staff, and families of officers and staff. Often times, they may visit officers and departmental personnel in hospitals, homes, and funeral homes.

Chaplains in law enforcement have many duties that relate to a victim or the community at large. In this arena, they counsel victims of crime and provide them with direct spiritual care. In the event of a disaster where large communities have been majorly affected, families need someone to aid them and direct them thru the chaos they have endured. Chaplains visit them, counsel the families, and bring them comfort. The Chaplain who visits these communities in distress communicates God's assurance, "Fear not, for I am with you" (Isaiah 41:10 NKJV) Spiritual care in the aftermath of major disasters can be feeding the hungry, clothing the naked, providing water for the thirsty, or sheltering the exposed. Once the person is met with their immediate needs then they will be in a mindset to be ministered. Law enforcement Chaplains fill a unique role in providing spiritual care, religious ministry, and intercession in the lives of many officers and support personnel who serve the public in crises and stressful situations.

Chaplains may be the only spiritual provider many officers and staff will ever know. With compassion, experience, and common sense, Chaplains counsel and encourage through availability, presence, nonjudgmental listening, and building trusting relationships by being dependable, honest, and transparent. Many agencies require specialized training, some of the courses are physical fitness, burn out and self-care, first aid, CPR, and critical incident stress management. Most training in law enforcement Chaplains however, focus on death and injury notifications and suicide prevention. Each agency has its own requirements, and even the experienced Chaplain has to go thru the agencies training program. [ii]

By (CI) Chaplain Norberto Guzman, B.A., M.C.C. / Signet Bible College and Theological Seminary

The Fire Chaplain

Many fire agencies recruit local clergy to serve as volunteer chaplains in order to handle emergencies within the department. The issues surrounding firefighters are similar to that of those who serve in law enforcement. This may include performing death notifications, counseling department personnel and their families, and ministering to department personnel during times of crisis. Fire chaplains also perform weddings, funerals as well as invocations and benedictions at academy graduations. Often, firefighter's tensions are heightened by the long hours spent in the fire station away from their families. The fire service becomes the second family for the firefighter adding stressors to the life of the emergency responder. Firefighters compete against their fellow firefighters for advancement. Shift work often leads to an increase in tensions.

Long periods are spent with coworkers in training, station and equipment maintenance, fire prevention inspections, and in highly intense emergency incidents. The adrenaline is often flowing just because they are on duty. This factor alone increases tensions as firefighters try to deal with each other and the public while the body is in a continual state of alarm.[iii]

Prison Ministry

Undoubtedly, correctional ministry requires a calling. The minister enters the world of locked doors, barbed-wire fences, armed guards, and painful solitude. They enter into the suffering of a defeated people who live with anger, depression, loneliness, hostility, and even despair. They penetrate the darkness of prisons while providing for the free exercise of religion for all inmates. In the tradition of Isaiah, they preach the good news of God's forgiveness and restore spiritual blindness. While inmates may face many years of incarceration, the minister releases the oppressed from emotional and spiritual prison of self-condemnation, anxiety, and bitterness.

Inmates suffer the same disappointments, hurts, and grief that others face outside the prison walls. They experience separation, broken relationships, and betrayal, demotions, disappointments, deaths, and deteriorating self-esteem; physical illness or disease, emotional turmoil or distractions, financial or economic hardships, and spiritual crisis. The difference between inmates and the average citizen is that inmates experience these things in complete isolation-separated from loved ones and support systems. The very nature of the circumstances makes them more vulnerable to emotional and spiritual distress. The environment within the correctional institution breeds many issues that intensify with the level of security of the institution. Jails, prisons, and penitentiaries all deal with inmates who succumb to peer-pressure while confined. The pressure to conform to the attitude of criminals or bad people is a coping mechanism for those who feel weak and vulnerable. The correctional minister is constantly dealing with the fear inmates have of being perceived as weak and exposed because they have chosen to make a lifestyle change, abandoning the life of criminal activity.

Inmates also deal with issues of depersonalization and dehumanization. They fear breaches of confidentiality, prejudice, and discrimination. For some, fear is the natural outcome of impending release, resettlement, or even execution. Correctional ministers have the difficult task of building trust with inmates through personalizing their relationships, humanizing their circumstances, equalizing their perceived inequities, and fostering peace and reconciliation in circumstance of prejudice, discrimination, racism and all forms of injustice.[iv]

The environment of the correctional institution is often a microcosm of the greater world of crime outside the bars, guarded walls, and monitored rooms of prison. Thus, it is particularly vital for prison ministers to understand the complicated nature of gangs, sexual assault, drugs, and crime. These are frequent issues inside prison walls, as well as in the world beyond.

In ministering to inmates, the Chaplain is called to provide compassionate care for people. In doing so, they are constantly assessing and making decisions about what approach to take. Respecting the boundaries of inmates while honoring his own boundaries may create tension for the Chaplain. How does the minister deal with this tension, and by what standards does he or she function? Boundaries are established for the mutual protection and accountability of the Chaplain and inmate.

Although there are moral principles that govern in a prison environment, a Christian Chaplain must use biblical principles when ministering to the inmate population. Institutions allow volunteer and Chaplain's minister to come in, in some cases however, they employ them. In any case, the Chaplain should apply biblical counsel in order to gain the trust of the people him or her ministers.

The prison Chaplain is committed to proclaim God's love to a people that may have never been to a church or heard God's word before. He steps in thru the prison doors and speaks God's word. Taking the initiative to meet people in their pain and suffering requires courage and compassion. He intentionally chooses to enter into the lives of people accompanying them on a journey that may include hardship as well as joy.

The prison Chaplain enters into an environment of differing cultures, interests and religions, therefore it is essential to have integrity and be compassionate in his character so that he could evangelize thru his walk. The work of a prison Chaplain begins with God's call to ministry. Every person experiences God's call in one way or another. It may be the call to saving faith or the call to faithful discipleship. By (CI) Chaplain Norberto Guzman, B.A., M.C.C. / Signet Bible College and Theological Seminary

The Hospital Chaplain

Hospital Chaplains offer ministry and spiritual guidance to patients, family members, and caregivers within the hospital setting. Many Hospital Chaplains work in an interfaith environment using a non-denominational style of counseling. They may perform specific religious duties related to the faith they were ordained in, for example, administration of last rites. Chaplains work with a diverse population, counseling patients undergoing surgical procedures, facing "end of life" issues or involved in traumatic accidents. They also offer comfort and support to patients' families. Hospital staff may call upon chaplains to calm angry or emotionally distraught friends and family members of patients. Chaplains may conduct religious services in the hospital chapel, including officiating at memorial services and weddings. In some cases, a Hospital Chaplain will provide spiritual support to fellow staff members and care providers.[v]

The Hospice Chaplain

Hospice chaplain duties pertain to the end of life needs of not only dying patients, but also their families, caregivers, community, and even the interdisciplinary medical team.

Hospice is more than just providing medical interventions during the end of life. Hospice Chaplains provide direct spiritual support and end of life counsel to patients and families in keeping with the spiritual beliefs of the patient and family. The goal of Hospice care is to enable patients to die with dignity, without pain, which includes meeting spiritual needs and social needs.[vi]

The Corporate Chaplain

Some businesses, large or small, employ chaplains for their staff and/or clientele. According to *The Economist (August 25 2007, edition, p64)* there are 4,000 corporate chaplains in serving in corporate America. Other chaplaincies outside of emergency services include rodeos, racetracks, fairgrounds, truck stops, clubs, and lodges. Typically, chaplaincy in these specific venues serve on a volunteer basis and contain the following duties but not limited to, performing opening invocations at major events, officiating weddings and funerals and ministering to personnel and their families. Truck driving chaplains often drive large rigs from truck stop to truck stop conducting church services for long-haul drivers. Usually, the trailer converts into a portable open platform allowing weary travelers to participate in church services while away from home. As in the case of the emergency service community, the chaplain spends time with personnel developing relationships and provides spiritual counseling to those in need.

The Three Levels of Chaplaincy

There is often the debate of what constitutes a professional chaplain and the expectation and role they should play in ministry. In some church settings, the role of the chaplain is seen as an offshoot of the church, an outreach designated for the sole purpose of ministering the gospel message. While this is ultimately the end goal, the duties of the chaplain will vary depending on industry needs and the requirements needed to fulfill those duties is at the discretion of each agency and institution.

The Professional Paid Chaplain

Most hospitals, state and federal agencies require their chaplains to have Ecclesiastical Endorsement and minimum of a Master of Divinity Degree (There are some exceptions) in order to function as a chaplain while local agencies tend to be more liberal on the matter and forgo the need for endorsement and higher education. When monetary value is placed on the chaplain, the requirements and expectations are much higher.

The Volunteer / Reserve Chaplain

Local agencies generally do not require endorsement or a graduate degree since they classify their chaplains as a reserve or volunteer personal. It is difficult to ask the local pastor of a congregation to volunteer his or her time and prequalify with graduate degree when there is no compensation for time and effort. Ironically, emergency services chaplains are often exposed to crisis situations such as shootings, suicides, in the line of duty death, and at times are faced with physical dangers that is customary in that line of work. The emergency services chaplain will periodically receive ongoing training in crisis management and safety in order to meet emergency services demands. The hospital or prison chaplain will rarely be required to respond to crisis situations other than that which takes place with in the hospital or prison setting. Though the emergency service chaplain is a non-compensated position, they are still classified as non-paid professionals. In comparison, a reserve police officer is required to undergo the same level of law enforcement training as a fulltime paid officer yet the reserve officer is a non-paid position.

Visitation Chaplains

Visitation chaplains *(Lay Ministry Chaplains)* typically volunteer their time meeting special needs at the county lockup, correctional facilities, assisted living facilities, hospitals and so forth. While a full time correctional chaplain will have to contend with the rigors of prison politics and life on the inside behind the walls, the visitation chaplain (volunteer) will only be tasked with providing the inmates with basic religious needs such as religious services, basic counseling and performing ceremonial duties. In hospital related ministries, the visitation chaplain will be tasked with visiting those who are sick and dying and will report directly to the on-duty (senior) chaplain. In most cases, these types of ministerial duties are usually part of a church outreach ministry with the goal of reaching the needs of the local community.

Three Levels of Chaplaincy

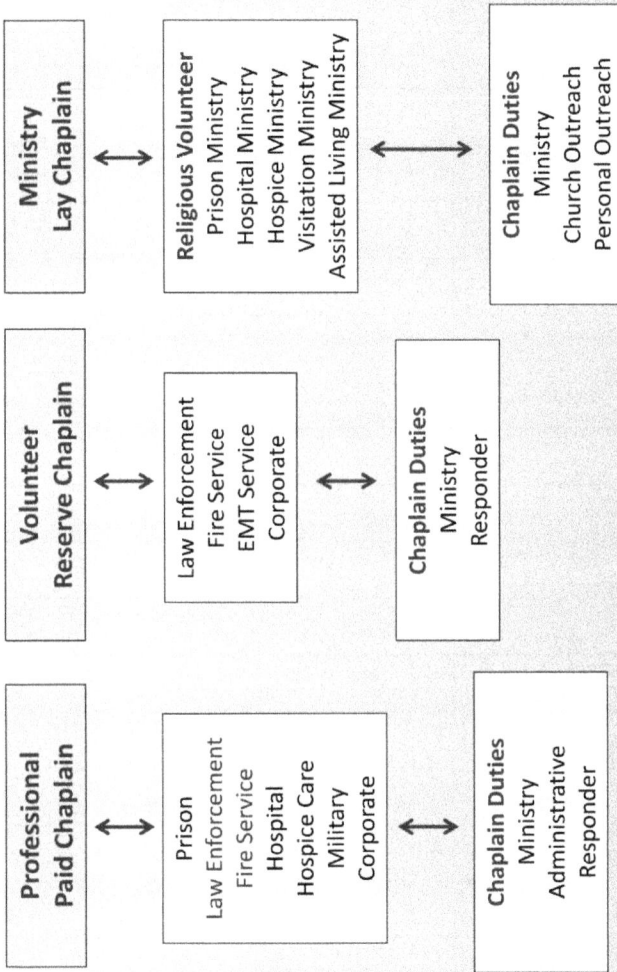

Professional Paid Chaplain

⟷

Prison
Law Enforcement
Fire Service
Hospital
Hospice Care
Military
Corporate

⟷

Chaplain Duties
Ministry
Administrative
Responder

Volunteer Reserve Chaplain

⟷

Law Enforcement
Fire Service
EMT Service
Corporate

⟷

Chaplain Duties
Ministry
Responder

Ministry Lay Chaplain

⟷

Religious Volunteer
Prison Ministry
Hospital Ministry
Hospice Ministry
Visitation Ministry
Assisted Living Ministry

⟷

Chaplain Duties
Ministry
Church Outreach
Personal Outreach

Student Notes

LESSON 2

Duties of the Emergency Service Chaplain

During times of crisis, as a chaplain, you may be asked to minister to people who are going through different types of emotional trauma. In the role of a chaplain, you are considered a caregiver as well as a spiritual advisor. However, unless you are also licensed as a professional clinician, you must remain in your field of expertise. In general, chaplains are ministers, not therapists, and even though what we provide as responders can be very therapeutic, most chaplains are not qualified to diagnose and treat medically related emotional issues. For the well-meaning chaplain, this can spiral into a legal quagmire that can result in both civil and criminal liabilities depending on the circumstances surrounding the incident if caution is ignored.

Agency Confidentiality

Most chaplains will be exposed to confidential information that is not for public consumption. More than likely the official agency will have a policy handbook, and the chaplain will be required to sign a confidentiality document restricting the distribution of departmental information. Confidential information is not to be shared with social media, news media, or the public. Most public agencies have a Public Relations Officer (PRO) who is assigned to update media and the public during newsworthy events. Never speak to the media unless you authorized or commanded to do so by your commanding officer or supervisor.

A Ministry of Presence

As clergy entering into the field of chaplaincy, we bring with us our religious concepts and ideologies. Religion and denominational debates can do major harm and destroy an established chaplain program undoing years of hard work and relationship building with departmental personnel. Often inexperienced chaplains enter the world of chaplaincy with the mindset of the church pastor and expect the same outcome when communicating with emergency service personnel that would be customary in a church setting. Protocols within the emergency services communities are much different from what is found within the walls of the local church.

Most agencies frown on proselytization unless invited to do so by personnel. In most cases, if proselytizing becomes an ongoing issue within the agency setting, the chaplain may be asked to resign his commission. The chaplaincy is a ministry of presence and is not a platform for recruitment to fill empty pews. Many people you meet may have different religious persuasions and the opportunity for evangelism may be non-existent. As a ministry of presence, Christ is demonstrated in our actions more so than public evangelism.

Providing Comfort During Crisis and Trauma

Shootings, suicide by firearms, and traffic accidents are common particularly in larger metropolitan areas where there is a higher probability that such events will occur. Hospital and hospice care chaplaincy though not as graphic as other type of service, still exposes the chaplain to those individuals who are sick and dying. When responding to a call for service, you will encounter many emotions. During times of tragedy, emergency service personnel are responsible for dealing with the matter at hand and often are unavailable to address those who are in crisis.

The victims perceive an adverse reaction by law enforcement officials as harsh and uncaring. Law enforcement when responding to the suicide, particularly if the suicide is a self-inflicted gunshot wound requires that the event and venue be treated as a crime scene even though there may be no evidence of an actual crime. In most cases, protocol requires that before a family can take possession of the body after a horrific event, the coroner's office must determine that no foul play has taken place. For family members, this can cause additional stress and anger towards emergency service workers. During this time, the chaplain can serve as a liaison between emergency services and the victim's family, providing updates and information when it is permissible. In many situations, victims may express anger towards the chaplain because of what they represent. Anger towards God is a temporary coping mechanism during times of tragedy. Such attacks should not be taken personally, as each victim may respond differently to traumatic events.

The following is a list of emergency callouts that are most common in emergency services chaplaincy,

Officer Involved Shootings

When an officer is involved in a shooting incident, in most cases the officer is placed on paid administrative leave. The officer is required to have limited contact with the general public including family until a review committee or the Office of Internal Affairs have the opportunity to debrief the officer and clear the officer of any wrongdoing. Such events are often an emotional time for the officer. The chaplain may be allowed to spend time with the officer and provide emotional support during this time of crisis. Most likely, the chaplain will be a member of the department, allowing the chaplain conditional access to the officer under review. In spite of recent media coverage of law enforcement involved shootings, it is an emotional and traumatic time for the officer.

In the Line of Duty Death

In the line of duty, death is one of the more stressful times for law enforcement and fire agencies. In addition to an already stressful work environment, the loss of a fellow officer or firefighter is not only traumatic for fellow responders and employees but the family of the fallen personnel as well. Your duties as an emergency services chaplain may include accompanying departmental command staff to the home of the officer and notifying the family of the death. Chaplains spend countless hours ministering to employees and are often involved in funeral perpetrations. Agencies, in larger cities, there are usually teams of chaplains within the department who will assist the lead chaplain with agency needs.

Visit Sick or Injured Department Employees

Chaplains are often called upon to minister to personnel who are injured on the job or who are facing a sudden illness. Ministry outreach includes ministering to the families of emergency services staff and departmental employees who have retired.

Callouts and War-Bags

Public service agencies rely upon chaplains to respond to emergency callouts. Larger cities who commission a large number of chaplain volunteers will usually have a callout system in place where a particular chaplain is assigned a timeslot and is on-call to respond on a moment's notice to emergency situations. Some agencies use a paging system or assign a department cellphone used for emergency purposes only. When responding to an emergency, chaplains should have ready a War-Bag with all the essential items necessary to provide services needed. A War-Bag is usually a black duffel bag that contains items that are used in the performance of your duties such as a high-quality flashlight, communion supplies if allowed, a notepad for taking notes and writing reports. Your wardrobe supplies should include a ball cap and extra polo shirt and a windbreaker with the designation of a chaplain on the front and backside of the jacket, rubber gloves, and emergency resource handout material. You may want to include in your arsenal of supplies items for children such as a small stuffed animal, coloring books crayons, and games, etc.

Other Major Incidents Include:

- ✓ Suicides / Suicide attempts
- ✓ Drowning accidents
- ✓ SIDS death*(Children)*
- ✓ Death by natural causes*(Old age and nursing homes)*

Crisis Intervention

Chaplains are taking a more active role within law enforcement agencies, fire services, hospitals and prisons serving as members of their in-house Crisis Support Team. They work with the Mental Health community conducting Critical Incident Stress Debriefing to first responders after a major event and provide aftercare. A major event includes natural disasters, in the line of duty death, aircraft, train and major car accidents just to name a few.

Notifying next-of-kin in death or serious injury incidents

Performing notifications are covered in greater detail in Lesson 5 of this training program and include,

- ✓ Notifications to the families of emergency services personnel
- ✓ Notifications to the general public (Death or accident)
- ✓ Notifications to the incarcerated (Prison inmates)
- ✓ Hospital notifications

Victim Assistances

It is beneficial for a chaplain to develop a working relationship with local agencies for referrals and resources. The chaplain should have available resources that can be handed out after a major incident where there are victims such as domestic violence, funeral resources, and public assistance materials. Local law enforcement agencies, county mental health, mortuaries, the Coroner's Office, local hospitals, the Red Cross and courthouses may be able to provide victim assistance handout material free of charge. You may be asked to do a follow-up and offer support for victims who are in crisis as well as provide additional counseling for families or individuals who are experiencing stress after an event. Support is typically done on a temporary basis until additional family, local clergy or other resources are made available.

Spiritual Guidance and Care

Chaplaincy is often demonstrated by action rather than by words and respect cannot be demanded, it must be earned. Earning and gaining the respect of emergency service officials is necessary to be efficient and have credibility as a chaplain. However, it is essential to be mindful of the religious and spiritual needs of the emergency service worker, and recommend them to their clergy when necessary. At times, it may seem that some emergency service personnel have no religious affiliation, never assume that their spiritual needs are not being met elsewhere. Emergency service workers have lives outside of their day-to-day work life, and many participate in local worship services in their community. In contrast, in the prison system due to their circumstances, and limited choices the incarcerated rely heavily on the chaplain and religious volunteers for their religious and spiritual needs and do so until their release date. However, public service chaplaincy has different protocols and expectations, and as a chaplain, you should be familiar with what they are and meet those needs accordingly. Remember, you are a guest in their backyard.

Other services provided include:

Care and Compassion
- ✓ Give confidential counsel to police personnel
- ✓ Be available to families of officers in traumatic situations
- ✓ Provide personal or family counseling

Special Events
Perform invocations and benedictions at Department functions such as:
- ✓ Promotion and award ceremonies
- ✓ Building and facility dedications
- ✓ Media events and inaugurations ceremonies
- ✓ Department academy graduations
- ✓ Preside at weddings/funerals

Student Notes

_____

_____

_____

_____

_____

_____

_____

_____

_____

_____

_____

_____

_____

_____

_____

_____

_____

_____

_____

_____

_____

_____

_____

_____

CHAPLAINCY 101

LESSON 3

Pastoral Confidentiality and Ethics

In recent years, there have been an increasing number of lawsuits filed against clergy for the invasion of privacy arising out of the disclosure of confidential information acquired during counseling sessions with parishioners. The result of these suits has brought about more scrutiny when it comes to confidentiality and the release of personal information.[vii]

Lawsuits for Breach of Confidentiality - Case History

The case history of Lightman v. Flaum, is one example of a violation of the clergy confidentially guidelines and sets a prescient for future lawsuits. In this case, the female plaintiff confided in two rabbis from the local Synagogue where she attended service. In her statement to the rabbis, she confessed was having an extra marital affair. The act of infidelity was a violation of rabbinical law. Thus, the two rabbis reported the conversation to plaintiff's husband,

which created additional stress on the already failing marriage.

Because of the breach of confidentiality, the plaintiff filed a lawsuit against the two rabbis for violating the clergy-penitent privilege rule. The rabbis argued the case filing and said it was bogus based on their perceived obligation as rabbinical leaders to report such matters. They also stated that they were allowed under the Religious Freedom Act to report such indiscretion to the plaintiff's husband. The trial court disagreed with the defendant's claims and sided with the plaintiff allowing the plaintiff to proceed with the lawsuit in the courts.[viii]

Mandated Reporter

There are exceptions to the rule. One example, where clergy confidentiality privileges do not apply is the matter pertaining to parent-child relationships. By 1974, all fifty states had mandatory reporting laws often referred to as "Child Protection Statutes." A crime perpetrated against minors, offer no clergy confidentiality privileges or protection from reporting a crime. Children are considered to have no voice thus are unable to defend or represent themselves as adults. It becomes the responsibility of the chaplain, pastor, Christian Education Director, children minister, and youth pastor to report any crime, suspected or otherwise.

Other clergy-penitent concerns involve confessions where the individual openly admits the intent to commit a crime, suicide or an act of violence. By law, clergy *(Mandated Reporter)* are required to report any individual who has expressed the intent to commit a criminal act particular when it involves violence. If while counseling an individual it is discovered that counselee intends to commit suicide, the pastor is obligated as a mandated reporter to report the threat. In general, the court system would prefer not to rely on testimony obtained by clergy while under the guise of confidentiality. However, the courts can make an official mandate requiring the pastor to reveal sensitive information if they deem it legally necessary. [ix]

Command Structure

Perhaps the most significant failure among individuals who serve as institutional chaplains is that they forget the cardinal rule that once the chaplain leaves the walls of his church and enters the world of institutional chaplaincy, they become guest of the institution and they can be replaced if departmental protocols are breached. Generally, there is a command structure in place be it in law enforcement, fire services or hospitals and is accompanied by rules and regulations by which the chaplain must adhere to if they are to achieve any amount of success among those they serve.

Personnel in every law enforcement agency, emergency response organization, hospital and prison facility answers to someone in authority. Many chaplains have been relieved from duty as a result of conflict with command staff or their insistent interference of departmental and institutional protocols as well as regulatory violations. A strong desire to minister the Gospel message often clouds the judgment of the chaplain because they approach the ministry from a church standpoint rather than an industry standpoint forgetting that the chaplain serves at the pleasure of the agency or institution. Most professional chaplains will be required to undergo orientation and training so that they become familiar with agency rules.

What is Ethics?

Ethics is the discipline, which guides our judgment concerning the morality of human acts. The discipline of ethics employs the power of human reason and all persons are bound in conscience to apply its principles to their conduct. Thus, ethics is a moral discipline dealing with human acts. Human acts are those actions performed by human beings, using their superior faculties of intellect and freewill, as opposed to those acts, which are common in the animal kingdom. Ethics is a discipline that studies the moral correctness of human behavior in relation to our natural end.

In summary, ethics is a science, which guides our judgment concerning the morality. "Morals" is human conduct in the light of principles. It is possible for a person to have good ethical concepts and bad morals, as in the case of someone who knows the principles but fails to apply them in concrete situations. Accurate, moral principles and good moral conduct are both essential. Ethics is also called "moral philosophy."

It is distinct from "moral theology" although they bear a close relationship to each other. Ethics is based on human reason alone, which looks only to a natural end, while moral theology (Christian ethics) relies on faith as well as reason, and recognizes a "supernatural end." Secular ethics/moral philosophy and Christian ethics/moral theology both deal with human acts. The formal object of moral theology, however, is the morality of the human actions towards a "supernatural end." As God is in control, we cannot choose a natural end but must strive to a supernatural end (according to God's will).[x]

Gratuity and Favors

Areas of ethical concern include the conduct of the chaplain on and off duty. As clergy, society tends to hold the minister to a higher standard, and there are regulatory rules regarding ethics within a departmental setting. Regulations concerning favors, gifts, and gratuities received by department personnel are frowned upon by law enforcement and fire agencies. In many instances, a chaplain in uniform walks into a coffee shop is offered a free meal or a substantial discount because of his emergency services affiliation. While the owner can provide the chaplain a free meal or discount as an act of kindness in recognition of his contribution to the community, the respective agency may view it as a gratuity in return for favors.

Chaplain Badge and Uniform

A chaplain misrepresenting his authority while in uniform and wearing a badge is considered a serious ethical breach. Chaplains International has a strict policy regarding official badge misconduct. This type of scrutiny of conduct holds true in law enforcement and fire agencies.

Representing oneself as a police officer is viewed as a serious violation of the law. A chaplain badge is a tool for quick identification during a crisis and other major events. Because most chaplain badges are designed using the same mold as badges used by police and fire departments, they can easily be misidentified as an actual law enforcement or fire department shield. Most police and fire agencies issue their chaplain's badges as a part of their uniform attire. For organizations that do not provide chaplain badges for their chaplains, organizational shields such as the ones issued by Chaplains International are often permitted to be to be carried on duty as an alternative to an agency shield. The organizational shield identifies the minister as a chaplain with Chaplains International. The title of chaplain assumes integrity and ethical conduct.

THE TEN COMMANDMENTS

The "Ten Commandments" is a summary of the principles of Natural Moral Law. Human beings could tell right from wrong even before God gave Moses the "Ten Commandments" because the natural moral law was already written in their hearts, as Paul teaches (Romans

2:15). Human hearts were drifted away from God, and He saw the need to get His Law before them more explicitly. The entire Natural Moral Law is not listed in the Ten Commandments.

The Ten Commandments only lists the major violations of natural moral laws addressing:

- ✓ The existence of God
- ✓ The worship of God
- ✓ Obligation to those in authority over us (God and parents)
- ✓ Sanctity of life
- ✓ Sanctity of marriage
- ✓ Conducts in living with others: (respecting the properties of others)

The Natural Moral Law is not meant to interfere with our liberty but guide us in the proper use of our freedom. The Ten Commandments are a set of God's directions on how we can avoid harm to ourselves and attain happiness both in this life and in the life to come.

Student Notes

_____

_____

_____

_____

_____

_____

_____

_____

_____

_____

_____

_____

_____

_____

_____

_____

_____

_____

_____

_____

_____

_____

_____

_____

_____

LESSON 4

Dealing with Suicidal People

Key Information

Estimates by the World Health Organization states that approximately 1 million people die each year from suicide. Suicide is a permanent reaction to a temporary problem, and any suicidal statements or attempts must be taken seriously. Say an individual confides in you and states he feels suicidal, you should do everything within your field of expertise to help that individual, including advising him/her to seek professional help immediately.

Responding to a Suicide Call-Out and on Scene Protocols

The Jumper or Man with a Gun

When approaching someone who is attempting suicide, the chaplain must approach with caution. Someone who is adamant about committing suicide can pose a danger to the chaplain as well as the emergency responder. If the person sees the responder as a threat, he or she may react negatively. A person with a gun may instinctively turn the gun on the chaplain or the responder then take his own life. When approaching the subject, it is important to remain calm and avoid excessive body movement such as the use of your hands while communicating with the subject. The subject may feel that you are approaching them with the intent of preventing them from the act of suicide and may react accordingly and complete the act. For example, a bridge jumper who has placed himself on the opposite side of the safety barrier may go through with the act of suicide if the person feels your motive is to apprehend him and prevent the action.

A person who is holding a gun to someone's head, or is standing on the edge of a rooftop threating to jump, is in full command of the situation. Many times a suicidal individual may feel they have gone too far and must go through with the act. The person may fear the possibility of incarceration, being held on a 72-hour hold as well as a loss of career and reputation. Do not deceive them but reinforce the idea that nothing has occurred that cannot be undone. The most powerful tool you have as a responder is communication.

Attempted Suicide - Do's & Don'ts

When communicating with someone who is suicidal, be mindful of your body language. Your body language can convey a message either positive or negative. For example, if you were to express your love for another person while shouting and shaking your fists, would the person view the gesture as a positive or a negative? Likely, from the person's perspective, the expression of love is overshadowed by the perception of contention and malice. The same is true when communicating with someone in a crisis. When approaching the subject, it is important to remain calm and avoid excessive body movement such as the use of your hands while communicating with the subject.

When communicating with the person, it is important to remain calm and if possible get the person to mirror you. Mirroring is a process of calmly and emotionally connecting with a person in crisis and getting them to pattern your behavior. Let us say a person is highly agitated and is experiencing anxiety. If your behavior is calm and peaceful, the person may unknowingly mirror your behavior. You may see a significant change in the person breathing, posture, and speech patterns. The idea is

INSTITUTE.

defusing the crisis and helping the person see that there are other options.

Zone of Safety

When responding to a suicidal person, the responder must maintain a certain distance from the individual to prevent the possibility of becoming a casualty of the crisis.

As a responder, you should never be so close to the person that they have the ability to grab hold of you causing you bodily harm. The distance between you and the person is extremely important when confronting a suicidal subject with a knife. If a police officer is confronted by someone with a screwdriver, in many cases the officer will shoot the suspect in self-defense. While a screwdriver may appear to be a less lethal weapon, it can be easily plunged into the victim and cause blunt trauma as well as death.

If something as simple as a screwdriver can cause great concern to the responder, then a person with a sharp object such as a knife should be handled with great care. In this scenario, the person may be holding the blade to their throat or in the case of a hostage situation, to the neck of the hostage. An individual attempting suicide with a firearm is going to be far more difficult to deal with

Page
49

because there is no safe distance by which you can position yourself other than taking cover behind a safety barrier.

Approaching a suicidal person with a weapon is usually going to be at the discretion of the responding agency. Other emergency personnel may be charged with the task of apprehending the individual to take control of the situation. However, it is not likely that you as a chaplain will be asked to assist. Therefore, your role is a ministry of communication, compassion, and presence.

Common Misconceptions about Suicide

People who talk about suicide will not really do it.
FALSE

Answer: Almost everyone who commits or attempts suicide has given some clue or warning!

Do not ignore suicide threats. Statements like "you'll be sorry when I'm dead," "I can't see any way out," — no matter how casually or jokingly said, may indicate serious suicidal feelings.

Anyone who tries to kill him/herself must be crazy.
FALSE

Answer: Most suicidal people are not psychotic or insane

They may be upset, grief-stricken, depressed or despairing, but extreme distress and emotional pain are not necessarily signs of mental illness. Major warning signs for suicide include talking about killing or harming oneself, talking or writing a lot about death or dying. A more subtle but equally dangerous warning sign of suicide is hopelessness. Studies have found that hopelessness is a strong predictor of suicide. People who feel hopeless may talk about "unbearable" feelings, predict a bleak future, and state that they have no future.

If a person is determined to kill him/her, nothing is going to stop them. **TRUE & FALSE**

Answer: Even the most severely depressed person has mixed feelings about death, wavering until the very last moment between wanting to live and wanting to die. *Most suicidal people do not want death; they want the pain to stop.* The impulse to end it all, however overpowering, does not last forever.

Talking about suicide may give someone the idea.
FALSE

Answer: **You do not give a suicidal person morbid ideas by talking about suicide**

The opposite is true—bringing up the subject of suicide and discussing it openly is one of the most helpful things you can do. *Source: SAVE – Suicide Awareness Voices of Education*

Suicide Prevention Starts by asking Key Questions

The first step is to find out whether the person is in danger of acting on suicidal feelings. Be sensitive, but ask direct questions, such as:

1. *How are you coping with what has been happening in your life?*
2. *Do you ever feel like just giving up?*
3. *Are you thinking about dying?*
4. *Are you thinking about hurting yourself?*
5. *Are you thinking about suicide?*
6. *Have you ever thought about suicide before, or tried to harm yourself before?*
7. *Have you thought about how or when you will do it?*

8. *Do you have access to weapons or things that can be used as weapons to harm yourself?*

Look for warning signs

You cannot always tell when a loved one or friend is considering suicide. However, here are some common signs:

•**Talking about suicide** — *for example, making statements such as "I'm going to kill myself," "I wish I were dead" or "I wish I hadn't been born"*

•**Getting the means to take your own life**, *such as buying a gun or stockpiling pills*

•**Withdrawing from social contact** *and wanting to be left alone*

•**Having mood swings**, *such as being emotionally high one day and deeply discouraged the next*

•**Being preoccupied with death**, *dying or violence*

•**Feeling trapped or hopeless** *about a situation*

•**Increasing use of alcohol** *or drugs*

•**Changing normal routine**, including eating or sleeping patterns

•**Doing risky or self-destructive things**, such as using drugs or driving recklessly

•**Giving away belongings** or getting affairs in order when there is no other logical explanation for doing this

•**Saying goodbye to people** as if they won't be seen again

•**Developing personality changes** or being severely anxious or agitated, particularly when experiencing some of the warning signs listed above - (By Mayo Clinic Staff)

How to Handle a Conversation or Phone Call with a Suicidal Person (By: David L. Conroy, PhD.)

---

1. **Listen, no matter how negative the conversation** may seem, the fact that it exists is a positive sign, a cry for help.

2. ***Be sympathetic, non-judgmental, patient, calm, accepting.*** *The caller has done the right thing by getting in touch with another person.*

3. *If the person says I am very depressed, I cannot go on, ask the question:*
   a. *Are you having thoughts of suicide?*

4. *If the answer is yes, you can ask additional questions:*
   a. *Have you thought about how you would do it? (PLAN)*
   b. *Do you have what you need? (MEANS)*
   c. *Have you thought about when you would do it? (TIME SET)*

5. *Simply talking about their problems for a length of time* *with suicidal people will often help defuse the situation.*

6. *Ask if the person has taken any drugs or alcohol,* *including prescription medication. If possible, get specific details.*

The most important pain-coping resource is the help of a trained mental health professional. A person who feels suicidal should get help, and get it sooner rather than later.

RECAP: SUICIDE WARNING SIGNS

Talking about suicide
Any talk about suicide, dying, or self-harm, such as:
- *"I wish I hadn't been born"*
- *"If I see you again..."*
- *"I'd be better off dead."*

Seeking out lethal means
Seeking access to dangerous objects that could be used in a suicide attempt such as:
- *Knives / Guns / Pills*

Preoccupation with death
- *Unusual focus on death, dying, or violence*
- *Writing poems or stories about death*

No hope for the future
- *Feelings of helplessness and hopelessness*

- *There is no way out and things will never get better or change*

Self-loathing, self-hatred
- *Feelings of worthlessness*
- *Guilt, shame, and self-hatred*
- *Feeling like a burden, ("Everyone would be better off without me")*

Getting affairs in order
- *Making out a will and giving away prized possessions.*

Withdrawing from others

- *Withdrawing from friends and family*

Self-destructive behavior

- *Increased alcohol or drug use and reckless behavior*

Sudden sense of calm

- *A sudden sense of calm and happiness after being extremely depressed can mean that the person has made a decision to commit suicide.*

Student Notes

_____

_____

_____

_____

_____

_____

_____

_____

_____

_____

_____

_____

_____

_____

_____

_____

_____

_____

_____

_____

_____

_____

_____

_____

LESSON 5

Death Notifications

Basic Death Notification Procedures

Death notifications may seem to some to be a simple concept, one with minimal consequences. However, such perceptions are dangerous and can do a great deal of emotional harm if performed incorrectly. There are basic rules of engagement, and if done correctly, the person being notified may recall the notification in the future as kind and compassionate.

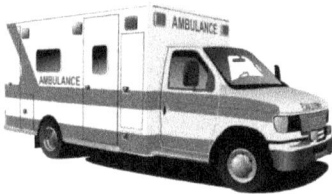

In Person

Always make death notification in person–not by telephone or police radio. Arrange for the death notification to be made in person, even if the survivor lives far away, either by contacting the Medical Examiner's Office or law enforcement agency.

Time and Certainty

- ✓ Provide notification as soon as possible
- ✓ Obtain positive identification of the deceased
- ✓ Notify next of kin and others living in the same household, including roommates and unmarried partners.
- ✓ Before the Notification-move quickly to gather information and bad death notifications have caused unnecessary trauma

Get the Facts

1. No one should learn of the death of a loved one from the media.
2. Be certain of the identity of the victim.
3. Determine the deceased person's next of kin
4. Gather detailed information, regarding the circumstances of the death

If Possible Do Notifications in Pairs

1. Always try to have two people present to make the death notification
2. Ideally, a law enforcement officer and a chaplain or a pair of chaplains[xi]

Take Separate Vehicles if Possible

1. Having two vehicles present provides flexibility
2. One chaplain may be able to stay longer to provide additional help
3. The team should decide who will perform the notification[xii]

USE Plain Language

1. The presenters should clearly identify themselves
2. Identify the survivor(s)
3. Present credentials and ask to come in
4. Remember, the presence of the team has already caused alarm so...
5. Do not make the notification at the doorstep
6. Ask the survivor (s) to be seated
7. Request that underage children leave the room
8. Young children should be notified separately if possible, and if requested by the family.
9. Give the death notification directly and in plain language
10. Call the deceased by name—rather than "the body."
11. Answer the survivor's questions directly
12. If you do not know the answer to a question, say so.

Compassion DURING CRISIS

Remember: Your presence and compassion are the most important resources you bring to a death notification. Remain sensitive to the survivor's emotions and your own. Never try to "talk survivors out of their grief" or offer false hope.

Be careful not to impose your personal religious belief with such statements as,

- *"It was God's will"*
- *"She led a full life"*
- *"I understand what you are going through"*

Give Survivors Helpful Guidance and Direction You can help the survivor(s) by offering to provide immediate assistance

Viewing the body

The survivor may want to view the body(s)

1. Survivors should be informed of the condition of the deceased's body.
2. Forensic restrictions that may apply

Death Notification in the Work Place

- Ask to speak to the manager or supervisor
- Ask if the person to be notified is available
- Ask the manager or supervisor to arrange for a private room
- Allow the survivor time to react to the news and respond with your support
- Let the survivor determine what he or she wishes to tell the manager or supervisor regarding the death

Death Notification in a Hospital Setting

The principles of death notification described above apply in the hospital setting. Here are several additional points: Find a quiet room in which the notification can be made and be certain the survivor(s) are seated.

(Do not make the notification in a crowded hall or waiting room.)

- ✓ If possible, arrange for a doctor to be present or available shortly after to answer medical questions or concerns
- ✓ Provide assistance and guidance

✓ Ask survivor(s) if they wish to spend time with the body of their loved one
✓ Refer the media to the investigating officer or victim service advocate
✓ Do not leave survivors alone
✓ Make certain someone accompanies them at all times
✓ Contact the survivor(s) the next day
✓ Optional: Make certain that the survivor(s) has your name and telephone number

Debriefing After a Death Notification

The Death Notification team members should meet as soon as possible afterward for debriefing.

Review the notification: what went wrong, what went right, and how can it be done better in the future. Share personal feelings and emotions. Death notifications are, without a doubt, stressful and often depressing. The notification experience may have triggered emotions.

Death Notification Specific to Suicide

It is important when performing a death notification it is done in a non-judgmental manner

Do not be afraid to use the word "suicide"

FOLLOW-UP:

If officer involved suicide, make contact with those closest to the officer.

Encourage co-workers to contact the deceased's family

It is extremely important for the survivors to try to put the "pieces" together to help better understand the events that lead to the suicide.

Expect Anger

- Do not be afraid to talk about the individual
- Reflect upon the way they lived, as well as the way they died

How Survivors Respond to Death Notification (Physical Shock)

Persons learning of the death may experience symptoms such as...

- ✓ Tremors
- ✓ Sudden decrease in blood pressure
- ✓ Shock is a medical emergency–help should be Summoned
- ✓ In many case the survivor may show no emotion
- ✓ Intensity of the event (I.e. violent death vs. heart attack)

Information

Attain as much information about the survivor's medical and emotional history before performing a notification. In the event that a survivor suffers from emotional or physical ailments, that is a consideration that must be factored into the notification process.

Other general reactions to death notification

Even if there is no physical or emotional response, the death of a loved one creates a crisis for the surviving family member(s).

Allow family members to express their feelings. Most likely, they will need help in determining what steps they need to take next. This may include additional notifications to other family members and funeral arrangements.

NATIONAL SHERIFFS ASSOCIATION – CHAPLAINS REFERENCE GUIDE

Student Notes

_____

_____

_____

_____

_____

_____

_____

_____

_____

_____

_____

_____

_____

_____

_____

_____

_____

_____

_____

_____

_____

_____

_____

_____

LESSON 6

Biblical Counseling 101

The concept of Biblical based Counseling centers on the belief that God through His written Word the Bible provides all the answers to life's most pressing concerns.

It is rooted in a Biblical understanding that God is the source of all knowledge necessary to heal and solve a person's problems.

Human problems are the reflections of a deeper spiritual condition from our inherited sinful nature. As Christians though we are purified at a spiritual level, we still battle with desires of the flesh.

The key for change is the process of progressive sanctification. We believe that the Bible provides answers for all of our sufferings. Today, we often think of counseling as the practice of psychology by therapists or clinical psychiatrists using extra-biblical theories and medical treatments. Sigmund Freud, the father of psychology *(meaning the study of the soul)*, defined it from a secular viewpoint and developed a medical discipline in treating the ailments of the human mind while ignoring the spiritual dimension. Biblical counseling is based on the concept that God can heal all people both spiritually as well as emotionally. The Word of God is not a cure to a problem rather it is embracing the heartbreaks of life from a biblical perspective and building a foundation for life on biblical principles and guidelines. There are circumstances where psychological intervention is necessary, and in such cases, a referral to a mental health professional is required.

Common Reasons for Seeking Counseling

There are times of turmoil and crisis in people's life when they realize that they are lost and cannot resolve their problems alone. Some of them cry out for help. These are times of vulnerability and sensitivity for the counselee. Asking for help takes humility because it is an admittance of personal failure, so Christian counselors need to be sensitive to these facts. Identifying the needs of the counselees is paramount.

There are Two Major Reasons for Seeking Counseling

Some are seeking (1) advice or (2) guidance on difficult or confusing issues. The following are some common reasons for seeking help:

✓ Family problems regarding children

✓ Marital problems

✓ Conflict resolution

✓ Drugs or alcohol abuse

✓ Sexual difficulty

✓ Difficulty at work/school/ career

✓ Moral or ethical dilemma

✓ Faith based issues

✓ Health issues

✓ Financial difficulties

There are two goals in Biblical counseling:

- **First goal** is helping the counselee understand their issues from Biblical perspective.
- **Second goal** is inducing the counselee to go through the Biblical process of change.

The Five -Step process of Biblical Counseling

STEP-ONE

Establishing relationship with counselees

STEP-TWO

Gathering important information about the counselee

STEP-THREE

Understanding the issues

STEP-FOUR

The Biblical process of change

Additional attachments included with lesson

Personal Data Inventory Form (PDIF) Extensive Data Gathering Question (EDGQ) Form

(The Five R's)

1. Responsibility for personal thoughts, attitudes, desires, feelings, motivations, words, and actions

2. Repentance for sinful thoughts and actions

3. Reconciliation with God and those involved by confessing the sins, asking for forgiveness and forgiving others

4. Renewal of the mind by developing an awareness of thoughts and actions that promotes sin; putting off desires, thoughts and actions that hinder biblical change; and replacing them with ones that promote biblical change.

5. Replacement of old habits with new good habits.

STEP FIVE

MAINTAINING CHANGE (Acronym "ACCEPT")

A – Acknowledge personal responsibility for thoughts and actions

C – Choose to live by biblical principles in all circumstances

C – Commit to a plan to eliminate whatever hinders biblical change

E – Execute the plan with energy toward the goals set

P – Persevere in obedience to Biblical principles

T – Trust God for the strength and resources for change

There are Two Major Types of Counselee

Counselors will find that when dealing with countless personalities of hurting people. Knowing the type of people we encounter will help us in choosing the approach appropriate for each.

The "talkers" - some counselees will quickly reveal lots of information. This type of counselee may provide seemingly unrelated or unimportant information to avoid talking about their real deep seeded and most painful issues. **The**

"reluctant" – Some counselees often are vague in their conversation requiring the counselor to pry with great effort, thus making it difficult to help them address their issues. Many people live in a state of denial in order to avoid dealing with the issue at hand.

We need to understand the causes for this reluctance

We need to understand reluctance from the counselee's point of view, not ours. Often, counselees are reluctant to share information because they feel embarrassed about their problems. *Some assume Christian counselors are righteous and perfectly holy people, therefore, would not understand them.* Some may be concerned that the counselors will pass judgment on them, will label or disrespect them. Others may not be forthcoming with information for fear that Counselors will betray their confidence and reveal their personal problems. *As a defense mechanism against ridicule or pain in dealing with certain difficult issues, counselees often put up walls.*

The counselor's task is to find an opening into the person's inner world where thoughts, anger, guilt and fears may be found. To be successful, the counselor must strive to remove those barriers by providing an environment where the counselee feels accepted.

Student Notes

LESSON 7

Establishing Relationships

In counseling, we must remember that the impact we make in people's lives has much to do with their perception of us.

Let us review the three building blocks needed to build a relationship

1. Empathy
2. Respect
3. Trust

Empathy

A relationship is established when people know that we sincerely care about them. People usually feel cared for when they are listened to and understood. Before responding to the counselee's issues, we should be seeking understanding about their circumstances asking the counselee questions and finding out what lead to the situation. It is important to ask open-ended questions and allow the person to share his or her story. Resist the impulse to quickly interpret their story and provide answers before acquiring all the details.

Be careful about using Christian clichés such as "It's all part of God's will" or "God lets things happen for a reason" can sound like insults to a person who has suffered deeply The fact that bad things happened for a reason is a conclusion the counselee have to reach on his or her own.

How are we to Show Empathy to Others?

Empathizing with someone requires us to be compassionate toward the person in his or her time of need.

Compassion is a trait that we, as counselors, should cultivate when ministering to the personal needs of others. The Bible gives us the following guidance in developing our compassion toward others:

- Think about how we would feel if we were in the counselee's position
- Treat the counselee as a family member
- Acknowledge our own capacity for sin
- Demonstrate genuine love and compassion toward the counselees

Many passages that refer to Jesus's compassion state first that He "saw" the people or He "looked upon" them.

Notice Luke's account of the mourning widow, *When the Lord saw her, (Jesus) He felt compassion for her. Luke 7:13*

Use Appropriate Non-Verbal Communication

Counselors should be conscious of their non-verbal language. The following suggestions provide guidelines for communication. Sit at the same eye level as the counselee as not to look down at them. Face the counselee directly indicates we are giving them our full attention. Relax arms, hands, and shoulders; avoid crossing arms in front. Lean slightly forward – communicates interest in what counselee has to say. Speak at a volume and intensity that reflects tenderness and compassion.

Good Eye Contact

Show interest by looking directly at the counselee, but do not stare. Avoid facial grimaces or expressions that communicate disapproval, anger or condescending.

Show Respect

One of the most important aspects of developing a genuine relationship with another person is by mutual respect for one another. Our counseling sessions can only move forward fruitfully when the counselee knows that we respect them regardless of what they have done in their lives.

Complete Honesty

We do not always have an answer to everything, but it is important to do our homework and give the best answer possible. Even if we have to stop and say, "That is a tough issue or question. I don't know the answer to that; but I am here for you. I am going to find out and get back to you with the answer. It is important to be truthful and honest not only to our counselee, but also to ourselves because God expects it.

Confidentiality

Confidentiality is the last hurdle to developing trust in establishing a relationship with the counselee. Counselors must keep all the information shared by the counselee in confidence. It is crucial that we clearly communicate to the counselees in words and with deeds that everything being discussed or shared are kept strictly confidential.

Diagnosis– Feelings

We are the sum of what we encountered in life and our reactions to these events. Being conditioned by life's experiences, we are prone to react to life impulsively and instinctively. Such actions reveal a man's inner life, his focus, and who and what determines the peace and joy in that person's life. Our usual focus is on what others have done or failed to do. As we maintain a defensive posture, we are inclined to judge, condemn, and criticize others. This self-focus is a breeding ground for anger, frustration, despair, bitterness, self-pity, and the like - a life of feelings. A feeling oriented life is a fertile area in which Satan operates and upon which he feeds. (1 John 2:3-6; Matt. 5:44; Gal. 5:19-21; Col. 3:5-9).

Doing

The ungodly live by their senses. Their lives are dictated by how and what they feel. This is what distinguishes a committed Christian from the world. A Christian lives by the will of God, not by feelings. However, there is nothing wrong with feelings in themselves until we act upon them. We are not to be directed or to live by feelings. We are to take stock and make note of our intents - the spirit that is being manifested. Then ask God for the grace to insure that we respond in a manner that honors and glorifies Him. Regardless of how we feel, we are to do what the word of God says to do. As we do to please the Father, godly feelings follow - the joy of the Lord. Living by the word, one serves God the Creator. Anything done without faith, without reference to God's word is sin. (James 4:17; Eph.

4:29; Rom. 2:6-9; John. 3:21; 1 John 2:3; Prov. 1:22-31; Rom. 8:13)

The Key

We establish godly roots by changing what we do in our lives and develop a strong union with Christ. This begins with the new birth, followed by daily renewal of the mind. Thus, life is confronted based on God's word - the will of God. As we do the word, the Holy Spirit changes our roots, which affects our feelings. This is a purification process, and we in turn, begin to respond to life in a manner that glorifies God (2 Cor. 10:3-5; Gal. 5:22-23; 2 Pet. 1:3-8; Eph. 4:22-24; Col. 3:10).[xiii]

Student Notes

LESSON 8

Anger/Guilt and Conscience

Some people have tried to make sense of their suffering by assuming that they deserve what they get, that somehow misfortunes is a form of punishment for our human sins. On the opposite extreme, there are many people today who choose to blame others or make excuses for their sinful behavior rather than being accountable for their actions. There are many examples in contemporary society to explain, lessen, normalize, or eliminate the facts or feelings of guilt. The explanations commonly used for the effects of guilt are excused by blaming the environment, sickness, or heredity. There appear to be concerted efforts to eliminate the impact of guilt by making sin seem normal.

The Definition of Guilt

Guilt is defined as a legal liability or culpability to punishment. The term guilt properly denotes the fact of responsibility and not the feeling that often accompanies it.

Negative emotions are a result of guilt. We can be truly guilty about something but not feel guilty. We must never minimize the "feeling of guilt" because there is always an underlying reason for guilty feelings.

Conscience

Conscience is a "warning sign" that reveals guilt. God has given us the faculty of the conscience to help us identify the presence of guilt. The word conscience means, "a knowing with" (suneidesis, Greek.) and has been defined as "the soul reflecting on itself." Our inner man uses the conceptual information we possess to evaluate our thinking and actions, much like a diagnostic program running perpetually on a computer.

Conscience reflects what we know or believe rather than what we feel. We may think something is right but feel hesitant or even hostile toward it, or we can feel right about what we know is wrong. The only solution to guilt is forgiveness through accepting Jesus as Lord and Savior in the lives of our counselees. Only God can remove the guilt of our sins through His appointed means of repentance. The counselor must be prepared to help the counselee work towards the goal of change and transformation to overcome their problems.

Identifying Feelings of Anger

Anger can occur for a variety of reasons however, chronic anger is a sign of deep-rooted issues that will require some digging to reveal the underlining truths that have created this abusive behavior. Angry feelings resulting from a major crisis may be a temporal emotion in response to painful stimuli. When we experience pain, loss, abuse, or hatred directed at us, we might feel angry. The feeling of anger is not sinful in itself. Anger is just an emotion. It is a temporal feeling. There are times when we are righteously angry, such as seeing injustice and senseless violence; but the expressions of that righteous anger can be sinful.

> *...be angry and do not sin, do not let the sun go down on your wrath, nor give place to the devil. Ephesians 4:26*

Anger can create a consuming environment where sin can flourish; if taken root, anger can lead to sinful deeds. Anger tends to isolate and separate us from others. Anger produces ungodliness and evil motives in us. Anger is sinful when it grows out of pride, hatred, jealousy and when it is expressed in sinful ways that hurt others or self. The DPP form is a useful tool for dealing with the topic.

Student Notes

CHAPLAINCY 101

LESSON 9

Gathering Information

Counselors are tasked with asking questions, listening, and gathering information. Counselors should avoid making assumptions before having all the available information. Otherwise, we risk making the counselee's situation worse, adding to their distress, or causing them to avoid biblical counseling in the future. During this step of counseling, counselors should encourage the counselee to do much of the talking while we listen and take notes. For successful biblical counseling to occur, a counselor must develop a skillful and organized method of gaining information.

Listening and Observing the Counselee

The Bible reminds us to "be swift to hear, slow to speak..." (James 1:19) and encourages us that "the mind of the prudent acquires knowledge and ears of the wise seek knowledge." (Proverbs 18:15). Counselors are not tasked to make an assumption, speculation, or judgment. The knowledge we are looking for has to do with facts. Getting the facts will require the use of the mind, in planning questions and methods, and the ears for listening. The most important skill needed by counselors is the ability to hear, which is at the heart of human communication. It is essential for the counselor to collect information. Good listening skills can be developed by listening to the counselee and not acting on assumptions.

> *Proverbs 18:13, states, He who answers a matter before he hears it, It is folly and shame to him"*

> *The heart of the prudent acquires knowledge, and the ear of the wise seeks knowledge. Proverbs 18:15*

The Need to Gather Facts

The above verse encourages counselors to listen and gather information from the counselee. Listen to how and what the counselee is saying in response our inquiries. We should expect three (3) responses from the counselee to our question about the issues. The answer can vary and may be superficial or vague.

The Counselor is tasked with Digging Deeper as Illustrated Below

Level one – The response by the person is vague without much detail.

- *"I am angry"*

Level two – This type of response reveals a particular trigger for the feeling or behavior.

- *"I am angry with myself because I hit my wife."*

Level three – This is the response we are looking for that sheds light on the underlying behavior pattern.

- *"I am angry with myself because I can't seem to control my temper when my wife tries to control me."*

Next, Counselors Need to Find Out What the Counselee Has Done About the Issue

Counselee could fail to recognize or understand the cause of why he/she behaves or feels this way. Counselors need to ascertain what the counselee wants the counselors to do about the issue. It is crucial for the counselor to understand the counselees' expectations of the counseling sessions. It is also important at this point to establish common objectives and goals with the counselee.

The Bible teaches us in Proverbs 18:15 that we are not to just listen passively to acquire information from the counselee; but it tell us to listen by actively seeking knowledge from the counselee that will enable us to answer them properly.

To Listen Actively, The Counselors Needs to:

Structure the sessions to elicit information

We are not just listening to a stream of consciousness talk driven by the counselee. Counselors must seek to clarify answers that are vague or superficial. We must listen for and elicit information that is specific to the topic.

Control the Flow of the Talk

Counselors must seek to acquire data that will address the issues at hand. Counselors must know what to ask, when to ask it, and how to word the questions in a prudent and wise way to retrieve the information.

Listen Beyond Attitudes and Feelings

Listening to the person is very important in obtaining information. Counselors should use reflective remarks and responses technique to get to information that is more specific.

Reflective Remarks and Responses Technique

The following technique will help the counselor to navigate the conversation. The following remarks are typical and sometimes vague.

Counselee's remarks - *"I can't"*

Counselor's responses - *"Do you mean can't or won't? - GOD says you can"*

Counselee's remarks - *"I've tried that but it didn't work."*

Counselor's responses -

- *Did you really try?*
- *How many times?*
- *For how long?*
- *In what way?*
- *How consistently?*

Get the details: What did you do precisely?

Counselee's remarks - *"I did my best."*

Counselor's responses - *"Are you sure? What exactly did you do that made this your best?*

Counselee's remarks - *"No one believes me."*

Counselor's responses - *"Think of one person who does or I believe you"*

Counselee's remarks - *"I could never do that."*

Counselor's responses - Never is a long time. Really how long do you suppose it might take to learn?

Counselee's remarks - *"If I had the time I'd do it."*

Counselor's responses - "You do. We all have 24 hours each day; it all depends on how you slice the pie. Now let's work on drawing up a schedule that honors GOD."

Counselee's remarks - *"Don't blame me"*

Counselor's responses - "You are saying you bare no responsibility"

Counselee's remarks – *"It's not my fault"*

Counselor's responses – "whose fault is it?"

Counselee's remarks – *"Don't ask me"*

Counselor's responses – "I am asking you, who else would know?"

Counselee's remarks – *"I guess so"*

Counselor's responses – "Are you really guessing or is it that what you believe or think?"

Counselee's remarks – *"You know how it is!"*

Counselor's responses – "Not really; can you explain it more fully so I can understand."

Counselee's remarks – *"I'm at the end of my rope"*

Counselor's responses – "Perhaps you are beginning to uncoil your problems for the first time."

Counselee's remarks – *"I have a need to!"*

Counselor's responses – "Is it a need or want or a habit?"

Counselee's remarks – *"I'm just one of those people."*

Counselor's responses – "Yes, I am sure you are, however Christ wants you to become a different person."

Counselee's remarks – *"That's just the way I am"*

Counselor's responses – *"Do you think that is how GOD wants you to be?*

Counselee's remarks – *"That's impossible"*
Counselor's responses – "You mean it is difficult."

Counselee's remarks -*"You can't teach an old dog new trick."*
Counselor's responses

Perhaps that is true but you are not a dog. You were created in the image and likeness of GOD! He knows you and commands you to change. The information we seek does not only come from words that we hear but also from information that is communicated non-verbally, known as

Student Notes

_____

_____

_____

_____

_____

_____

_____

_____

_____

_____

_____

_____

_____

_____

_____

_____

_____

_____

_____

_____

_____

_____

_____

_____

_____

LESSON 10

Para - Linguistic Communication (Halo Data)

Halo Data has to do with the manner in which a counselee speaks - not what they say, but how they say it. The tone of voice, the hesitation, and choice of words can reflect their emotional states, how they feel deep down.

Behavior - *Genesis 3:8 says ...*"the man and his wife hid themselves from the presence of the LORD GOD among the trees of the garden."

This type of action reveals important information about what the person is feeling. They do not have to say one word for us to know that they were experiencing the guilt and fear that come from sinning.

In Counseling, we can Learn Much from the Body Language of the Counselees

Facial expressions will show discomfort when certain topics are discussed, reactions such as anger, sorrow, or other emotions. Sometimes counselees will involuntarily cross their arms in front of their chest or fidget uncomfortably when dealing with certain issues. They may also divert their eyes toward the floor or avoid eyes contact when Counselors mention a particular issue.

Halo Data can also provide material for questions for example:

- *"When I asked you that question you seemed uncomfortable. Could you help me understand what bothered you about the question?"*
- *"You seem upset today. Was it something I had said or done?*
- *"You seem a little preoccupied. What are you thinking about?"*

Productive Questioning

Counselors should be aware to ask questions that encourage the counselees to do most of the talking and revealing their true feelings, thoughts, and the motivation for their actions.

Avoid Questions that Start with "Why"

Usually, a question that begins with the word "WHY" tends to evoke speculation and put people on the defensive because it makes them feel challenged.

Ask More of the "What" Type of Questions

Generally, what type of questions produce much more information than why questions.

- What is the problem?
- What happened?
- What do you mean?
- What have you done about it?
- What has helped?
- What made it worse?
- What do you think about it?

Helpful Questions Start with the Word "How"

- "How do you feel about it?"
- "How have you responded?"
- "How have you reacted?"
- "How have you tried to resolve it?"
- "How long have you had this problem?
- "How often have you had it?"
- "How can I be of help?"

The how questions invite the counselees to open up, to express them and reveal their true feelings.

Avoid Questions that can be answered with "Yes" or "No"

Counselors should ask "open-ended" questions, so that the counselee does not answer with a yes or a no.

The following are examples of open-ended questions

Instead of: *"Do you want to get married?"*
Ask, *"What are your thoughts about marriage?"*

Instead of: *"Do you love your husband?"*

Ask, *how do you feel about your husband?*

Instead of: *"Are you satisfied with your job?"*

Ask, *"What do you like or dislike about your job?"*

Student Notes

LESSON 11

Personal Data Inventory Forms (PDIF)

The Personal Data Inventory forms are designed as both a counselor and counselee as a resource and are an essential tool for learning about the persons likes and dislikes religious worldview, personality traits, marriage, and health information. While it may seem somewhat invasive, information gathered can provide critical material that can expose deep-rooted truths and links to a troubled past. Relevant information such as a person's physical and mental health can be an obstacle to resolving stressful difficulties.

For example, a person who has experienced a sudden death of a loved one may suffer a time of deep depression as they mourn their loss. The individual who has suffered a significant loss must take emotional steps to reconcile him or herself to the fact that this is the close of a chapter in the life of the person who is going through this time of significant trauma. The recovery process takes time does not come with a set deadline for emotional recovery and the spiritual caregiver must stand ready to provide comfort to the person who is going through this time of emotional suffering. If the person who is suffering the loss is in the same emotional state of mind a year following the death and there are no noticeable signs of recovery, then there may be something much more profound and physical to consider. The spiritual counselor may be equipped to address the person in crisis from a scriptural perspective. However, a person who is rooted in depression for an extended period may be suffering from a chemical imbalance that can only be resolved by medication.

If while interviewing the counselee it is discovered that the individual has not received care from a medical professional, then it may be incumbent of the counselor to recommend the counselee to seek a medical checkup before undergoing a lengthy counseling session. The person who is a suffering chemical imbalance as a result of emotional stress is not crazy but somewhat clouded by a lack of hope. While providing spiritual care is the right passages to recovery, a person who is dealing with a chemical imbalance will be distracted by feelings and a sense of doom. A person's physical condition must first be addressed and corrected before moving on to the next stage of spiritual counseling. The DPP form will help in retrieving crucial information that will not only provide a synopsis of the person's life, but it can also reveal underlying medical issues that can hinder the recovery process.

Information Collection Tools [See Appendix 1]
Now we will look at the tools and techniques that we can employ to help us gather information in an organized and methodical fashion.

Primary tools

(1) Personal Data Inventory Form (PDIF) – see Appendix 1
(2) Extensive Data Gathering Questions – see Appendix 2

The Personal Data Inventory Form can be provided to the counselees during the initial encounters as homework for them to fill out on their own time. This can be done before the next counseling session.

PDIF can be a useful tool in the initial stages of counseling for the following reasons:

- Requiring that counselees complete a PDIF indicates a counselor's concern for thoroughness.

- The form provides constant access to basic information that the counselor may forget or neglect to cover during the counseling sessions.

- The information helps to prepare the counselor for the counseling sessions. It will often reveal the initial direction the counseling should take.

- Completing the form help counselees think about the issues that will be discussed.

- Discussing information from the form with the counselee can provide a natural and appropriate entry point into the counseling session.

Identifying the Issues

Our worldview is defined as our personal model, theory, assumption, interpretation, and frame of reference for the world around us. It is the way we "see" the world and it influences our attitudes and thoughts, and leads us to certain choices and behaviors.

Example

Two people could be looking at the same identical facts and they would both acknowledge these facts but each person's interpretation of these facts represents their prior experiences, and the facts have no real meaning whatsoever apart from the interpretation or perception. Negative experiences from certain people, places, and circumstances in our past sow the seeds for the negative thoughts, perception about life, personal feelings, and daily behaviors. By identifying and addressing, the problem at the core provides the steppingstones towards reconciliation.

CHAPLAINCY 101

Appendix 1 – PERSONAL DATA INVENTORY FORM (PDIF)

IDENTIFICATION DATA:

Name   Birth Date

Home Address

Email   Facebook

Occupation

Marital Status: Single   Unmarried, Domestic

Partnership   Engaged   Married

        Separated   Divorced   Widowed

other, (explain)

Education: Grade   High School/GED

College (degree   )

Graduate (degree   )

Other training (list type and years completed)

HEALTH INFORMATION:

Rate your health (check):   Excellent   Good

        Average   Declining   Poor   other,

explain

Weight changes recently: Lost   Gained,   Your

present weight

List all important present or past illnesses or surgeries or

injuries or handicaps:

Date of your last medical examination:

Report:

Are you presently taking medications?   Yes   No,

What?

Have you used drugs for other than medical purposes?

        No,   Yes

(If yes, please explain)

CHAPLAINCY 101

Have you ever had severe emotional breakdown?

    No   Yes, explain

Have you ever been arrested?   Yes   No, explain

Have you recently suffered the loss of someone who was close to you?   Yes   No, explain

Have you recently suffered loss from serious social, business, or other setbacks?   No   Yes, explain

MARRIAGE AND FAMILY INFORMATION

Name of spouse

Date of Birth   Age   Sex   Height   Weight

Home Address

Email

Occupation:

Spouse's religious preference

Is your spouse willing to come to counseling? No

Yes   Unsure

How long did you know your spouse before marriage?

Length of engagement

Your ages when married: Husband   Wife

Date of marriage:

Location of the marriage ceremony:

Have you ever been separated? Yes   No

When?

Have either one of you or your spouse been married previously

or had children from other relationships?   No   Yes

If yes, please give brief information about them:

Information about the children:
Previous Relationships (Name)

If you were raised by anyone other than your biological parents, briefly explain:

Did your parents divorced before you were 18 years old?

     Yes   No

How many older brothers   sisters   do you have?
Describe your relationship with them

How many younger brothers   sisters   do you have?
Describe your relationship with them

Do you have any half siblings?   Yes   No

Do you have any siblings from your mother or father previous

marriages?   No   Yes, explain

PRESENT ISSUE

PLEASE BRIEFLY ANSWER THE FOLLOWING QUESTIONS ON

SEPARATE SHEET OF PAPER:

1. What is the nature of your problem?
2. What have you done about it?
3. How long have you had this problem?
4. What prompted you to seek help now?
5. What can we do? (What are your expectations in coming here?)
6. As you see yourself, what kind of person are you? Describe yourself.
7. What, if anything, do you fear?
8. Is there any other information we should know but did not ask on this form?

Review of Topic

Our subjective interpretation of the world around us or our "worldview", rightly or wrongly, directly colors our perception, attitudes, feelings, thoughts, and behaviors, which in turn affect the way we interact with other people and circumstances. Our worldview often is the root cause of our problems.

We all created our worldview through the totality of our experiences, the good, bad, hurtful, joy, disappointments, fulfillments etc. Some powerful and impactful or repeated experiences in our life conditioned us to respond a certain way. These powerful conditionings affect the way we see the world.

Negative experiences from certain people, places, and circumstances in our past sow the seeds for the negative attitude, perception, feeling, thinking and behaviors today. Our experiences conditioned us to respond in a certain way. If these conditionings resulted in repeated behavioral responses, they become patterns or habits overtime. Gathering DPP information is useful for discovering a pattern of behavior or habit and its triggers. This will help both counselors and counselees in mapping out a strategy for altering counselees' worldview which will resulting in breaking and replacing habits, avoiding occasions or triggers for sinful activities at the later stage of biblical counseling. This will be discussed in further details as we continue to explore this chapter.

Discovering Problem Patterns (DPP)

Counselors may use a tool called "Discovering Problems Patterns" (DPP) Journal Form (see appendix 3), as a homework assignment for the counselee to complete (For a period of one to four weeks) and to help uncover specific behavioral patterns. For instance, a counselee may be dealing with anger as mentioned earlier. The counselee should keep a DPP journal to determine the triggers that lead to the emotional outburst. The counselor may discover the counselee's daily habits may be associated with a time of day, fatigue, alcohol consumption, and arguments with friends or family. Gathering such information is useful for discovering a pattern of behavior or habit and its triggers. Knowledge will help both the counselor and counselee in mapping out a strategy for altering counselees' worldview, which will result in breaking and replacing bad habits, avoiding occasions, or triggers that lead to a continuation of the problem.

Using resource material

The Discovering Problem Patterns form and the Taking Thought Captive Worksheet are two excellent resources that can be given to the counselee as homework assignments that will help them work through behavioral issues. The DPP form helps the counselee discover and document events leading up to specific patterns of behavior so that they can be appropriately addressed.

Taking Thoughts Captive Worksheet is a useful resource for the counselee in addressing documented behavioral issues and taking corrective action, and both forms can be modified as needed to meet counseling needs. The resource forms can be used to address a variety of behavioral situations, and by using these resources, the counselee will learn to identify triggers that lead to outburst emotional distress and can help the person take the necessary steps to control destructive behavior.

While some of the techniques recommended in this course of study are designed for use in more control setting, principles can be utilized when verbally counseling the individual. For example, when conversing with someone in law enforcement who is seeking advice regarding a personal issue, one that leads an emotional outburst, the counselor can ask the person what triggered the event and why was the person unable to control his or her emotions.

DISCOVERING PROBLEM PATTERNS FORM (DPP)

APPENDIX 3

Name:

_____

Direction: For one week carefully list events, situations or activities that resulted in behaviors that caused problems

_____

Circle the days the behaviors occurred. Then document the time of day, circumstances, feelings, thoughts and desires that led to the behavior.

Sunday   Monday   Tuesday   Wednesday   Thursday   Friday   Saturday

Morning:

_____
_____
_____

Afternoon:

_____
_____
_____
_____

Evening:

_____
_____
_____

Taking Thoughts Captive Worksheet
Appendix 5

Name: _____ Date: _____

1. What is the thought which is concerning to you that needs to be addressed or changed?

    _____
    _____
    _____
    _____
    _____
    _____
    _____
    _____
    _____
    _____
    _____
    _____
    _____

2. What are the circumstances that gave rise to the thought that concerns you?

    _____
    _____
    _____
    _____
    _____
    _____
    _____
    _____
    _____
    _____
    _____
    _____
    _____

3. What is God's truth on this subject(s)? (*Write out verses from your study or the counsel of others.*)

4. What is the concise prayer that you pray when the thought arises? (*thanksgiving and request*)

5. What specific actions will you take concerning your circumstance or thinking?

Student Notes

LESSON 12

Biblical Process of Change

The unique ability of self-awareness helps us determine whether our perceptions are reality and principle-based, or they are just carnal feelings based on the past. We do have the freedom to choose our reactions based on carnal feelings or rely on the principles set forth by God through His written word.

Carnal Feelings vs. God's Will

We must help the people we counsel understand that a person and their past lifestyle, is always accompanied by a closet full of consequences.   We cannot change the person we used to be. We can only become the person God wants us to be and the person we should have been.

In this portion of the lesson, we will present five steps necessary for change also known as the "Five-R's" of Biblical Change:

A. **Responsibility**

B. **Repentance**

C. **Reconciliation**

D. **Renewal of Minds**

E. **Replacement**

Prerequisite for successful change is personal encounter with Jesus Christ. Real change does not come from a person, a method or a program. It comes from developing an encounter and a relationship with Jesus.

If we sense a need for the counselees to accept Jesus as their Savior and Lord, this is the time to settle this matter with God before we go on. Pray to God with the counselees and ask God to speak to them as counselors guide them through the following scripture passages:

- *Romans 3:23 – All have sinned.*
- *Romans 6:23 – Salvation and eternal life is a free gift from God.*
- *Romans 5:8 – Because of His love for you, Jesus paid the death penalty for your sins.*
- *Romans 10:9-10 – Confess Jesus as your Lord and believe that God raised Him from the dead.*
- *Romans 10:13 – Ask God to save you, and He will*

Responsibility

Current social science tells us we are the product of our social conditionings and circumstances. This perception seems to excuse us from being responsible for our thoughts and actions, but our conscience says otherwise. On the one hand, we acknowledge the power of conditioning in our lives; but to say that we are determined by it or that we have no control over those influences lessens our humanity with God given freedom to choose.

There are three (3) major excuses that are widely accepted to explain the nature of man today.

- **Genetic** – I am the way I am because of my genes. It is the genes I inherited from my family.

- **Psychological** – My childhood experiences essentially determine my character and personality.

- **Environmental** – Someone else or something else in my environment (social and economic situations, national law/policies) is the cause for our behaviors.

Elements of True Repentance

Confessing – There is a two-fold nature of inward confession that is revealed in the meaning of the Greek verb *homologeo*("to say the same thing"). First, we must acknowledge to ourselves and to God the fact that we are sinners. Second, we need to agree with God about the nature of our sin.

Choosing – True repentance always includes a willful resolution not to repeat the sin.

Renewal of Mind

We have to go through a shift in our worldview, the way we see and perceive the events around us. The Bible calls this shift "renewal of mind." This experience is common to "born again" Christians. The "renewal of mind" experience can create powerful changes because we see things differently. We see things from a Godly perspective. It becomes obvious that if we want to make relatively minor changes in our lives, we can focus on our attitudes and behaviors. However, if we want to make significant quantum-leap changes, we need to work on shifting from our temporal, experiential, conditioned and inaccurate worldview to Biblical principles.

Maintaining Change – Review

The plan for continuing changes and transformation is by following a process **(using acronym "ACCEPT")**

A – Acknowledge responsibility for our thoughts and actions.

C – Choose to live by biblical principles

C – Commit to a plan to eliminate whatever hinders biblical change

E – Execute the plan with energy toward the goals set

P – Persevere in faithful obedience to Biblical principles

T – Trust God for the strength and resources for change

CHAPLAINCY 101

Student Notes

LESSON 13

Critical Situational Stress

Critical Incident Stress Debriefing (CISD) is a technique designed to minimize the impact of a traumatic event and to aid in and emotional recovery. Dr. Jeffrey T. Mitchell, of the University of Maryland, designed "critical incident stress debriefing" to prevent post-traumatic stress among high-risk occupational groups. Initially developed for firefighters, paramedics, and police officers, use of the Mitchell Model has been modified and expanded for use in natural disasters.

Critical Situational Stress is a Normal Reaction to Highly Abnormal Event

Critical Situational Stress is a normal reaction, in ordinary people, to highly abnormal events. If left untreated and allowed to fester, it can become detrimental to the counselees. When properly handled, this experience can lead them to renewed spiritual awareness, redefined value systems and priorities, and new insights, which can foster growth into a new direction in their lives. Life presents many unexpected changes that bring on severe situational stress on the counselees that Christian counselors might face; News of terminal illness, death or serious injuries to loved ones.

Grief and Bereavement – recent death of family members or loved ones

Example of major losses

- Recent divorce or separation
- Financial loss,
- Loss of employment
- Accidental Death
- Suicides

Severe depression needs referral to healthcare professionals.

What is Critical Situational Stress?

Critical Situational Stress is the normal physical, mental, and emotional reactions that go along with the acute loss. Untreated, this stress response can lead to isolation and anger and can affect physical health, marriages, family relationships, employment and even faith in God. Counselors are called to be God's instruments for healing by ministering to the brokenhearted and in binding up their wounds. In the following chapters will provide the counselor with a structured introductory training program to help better understand and assist the counselee who is going through general critical situational stress.

Counseling During Critical Situational Stress

1. The goal is to alleviate the effects of acute stress symptoms by providing support emotionally, physically, and spiritually through:

- *Spending time with the sufferer*
- *Listening and being non-judgmental*
- *Pray with the sufferer*
- *Provide resources and educate*
- *Helping them with their family members, i.e. children*

2. Assist them through the normal recovery process by helping counselee succeed through the four phases of dealing with major loss and stress.

Phase 1 – Accept the reality of the loss.

Phase 2 – Freely experience the pain of loss.

Phase 3 – Adjust to the new environment after the loss by making changes.

Phase 4 – Move on with life.

---

3. Identify those who need a referral to mental health professionals

---

Preparatory Checklist for Debriefing

Counselors must prepare before the start of a debriefing session. The following is a checklist and is useful when preparing for a debriefing session.

Location

- The session should be accessible only to approved parties
- No distractions or interruptions such as cell phones, texting, or radio traffic
- Adequate and comfortable seating
- Proper room temperature
- All pagers, cell phones, radios must be off or in silent mode

- When providing childcare, it should be held in a separate location.
- Have refreshments available (Fruits, bagels, muffins, water, juices, or herbal teas)
- Have handout materials available

Debriefing
CRISIS SITUATIONAL STRESS

One - Introduction Phase

Introduce yourself as a Christian counselor from **(Your Church)**. Explain your role as Christian counselor during the debriefing process. Establish ground rules for the sessions. Assure all in attendance of the rules of confidentiality.

- Let those in attendances know that this process is not psychotherapy.
- Encourage participation and mutual support, but assure them that they are not required to speak.

This only a sample of questions you may ask during a debriefing. Some people in attendance may or may not be religious and questions about their faith and spirituality may not be applicable.

Two - Fact-Finding Phase
Ask about the crisis:
- *"How were you notified?"*
- *"How did you hear about it?*
- *"Where were you?"*
- *"What role did you play in the event?"*

Three - Gathering Thoughts Phase
- *"What were your first   thoughts?"*
- *"What was your immediate concern?"*

Four - Understanding Reactions Phase
- *"What part of this crisis bothered you the most?"*
- *"As you look back over what happened, what part of the crisis stood out the most?"*
- *"What would you do different?"*

Five - Identifying Symptoms Phase
Provide examples of psychological, physical, emotional, behavioral changes as well as changes spiritually.
- *How has this affected you?*
- *What was it like for you during the first days after the event?*
- *What was it like for your family members, children?*

- *How has this affected your personal and your family relationship?*

Six - Teaching Phase

Teach to the symptoms identified (personal and other family members) Provide Stress Management Principles and Strategies (see next section and handout Appendix 7) Reinforce the concept of "being there" Provide additional teaching materials specific to the event.

Seven - Re-Entry Phase

Introduce any new material if appropriate at this time Review education material, provide appropriate handouts Network participants into additional resources such as groups of people with similar experiences Answer questions, reassure and inform as needed.

Common Immediate Stress Reactions

People involved in an emotionally charged event may be experiencing normal stress responses to it. The signs of critical situational stress can be manifested physically, emotionally, cognitively, and behaviorally. These stress responses can occur immediately, within hours, days or even weeks. Each person will respond to stress differently. Counselors should be aware that eighty-five percent (85%)

of all people exposed to severe loss might develop noticeable stress symptoms within 24 hours. Some may experience an immediate stress or grief response, or a variety of stress symptoms, or may not have any of these reactions right away.

Counselors can reassure counselees that the effects of critical situational stress are completely normal.

These are normal responses to an abnormal event. For some people these symptoms will dissipate within two weeks. If symptoms worsen, or if they do not begin to dissipate after week two additional intervention by medical professionals is warranted.

When interacting with counselees in crisis we may notice the following symptoms

Tension – physical and emotional tension, muscle tremors or twitches, and restlessness

Fatigue – decreased energy

Sleep disturbances – insomnia, bad dreams, or nightmares

Diet – change in eating or drinking habits

Nausea – nausea, vomiting other gastrointestinal problems

Recurring feelings

- Sadness
- Helplessness
- Anxiety
- Anger
- Discouragement
- Frustration
- Vulnerability
- Depression
- Guilt
- Self-blame
- Insensitivity
- Blaming others

Spiritual Reactions

- Question belief systems and a decrease in spiritual activities
- Question good vs. evil "Why did God allow this to happen?
- Question one's own values
- Angry at God
- Abandon spiritual beliefs Blame God

- Spiritual isolation from others Loss faith in God
- Over compensation to spiritual beliefs

Stress - Management Principles

The following are some basic stress management principles that have been shown to help reduce the symptoms of severe situational stress that counselors could provide for counselees.

- Eat nutritious foods: fresh fruits, vegetables and balanced meals
- Get some physical exercise to reduce some of the physiological effects of stress
- Moderate intake of caffeine
- Avoid alcohol or other depressants
- Rest well by getting adequate sleep (at least 8 hours per night)
- Engage in relaxing activities such as walking, stretching, listening to music
- Find time to do things the counselees enjoy such as hobbies, play musical instrument, gardening, etc.
- Avoid changes in counselees daily routines
- Do not make any significant life altering decisions while still stress

- Find friends or a support source to talk to about the incident.
- If the symptoms of stress do not lessen, seek additional intervention.

Student Notes

LESSON 14

Traumatic Stress Reactions and Children

Most people, including children, react to traumatic stress in a typical pattern. Specialists agree that for the most part, people in time adapt to personal loss. In general, younger children follow a pattern similar to that of adults; however, children's level of cognitive development limits their initial understanding.

Children tend to move cyclically between three basic postures: Distress, withdraw or shut down their awareness and responses.

Children may return to normal activities while seemingly oblivious to the situation. Unlike adults, children can only accept as much as they can process cognitively and emotionally. Adults attempting to talk to children about the incident may be met with mixed responses. While sometimes such efforts are well received, more often they are ignored or scarcely tolerated.

Children may just stare blankly, walk away, change the subject, or act out. They may appear to be in denial when in fact they are simply baffled by surrounding adult behaviors, parental absence, and change in routine.

Younger children tend to exhibit clinging behavior and separation anxiety following traumatic stress.
Children sometimes approach the subject as they would an unsolvable puzzle, making repeated attempts to fathom its meaning.

Mid-childhood-age children tend to show distress more directly, going through periods of more obvious suffering. If the pain is too great, they may withdraw and deny the emotional reality of the traumatic experience to others or even to themselves. Their feelings often appear blunted; and when they discuss the incident, they tend to do so in a detached manner. They "play out" their distress through games, fantasy, acting out behavior and reflection.

Adolescents often talk about the traumatic incident in a straightforward manner. They express immediate emotions overtly but show deep feelings indirectly and often in self-destructive ways.

Children reactions parallel those of adults, with the exception that they reflect adolescent developmental issues. One minute they may discuss the incident with appropriate expression of feelings, the next day they may act out in a childish manner. One moment they may want to be near their parents, another moment they may be caught up in an outburst of peer-group hysteria.

The more serious the trauma, the more the child may exhibit symptoms of stress and withdrawal. The nearness of the incident may have an effect on the child, whether it is an event that they were personally involved in or an event that a parent or family member experienced. Many of these reactions are a form of Acute Stress Response (ASR). Suggestions for coping strategies for parents include having them recall what has worked for their children in the past.

Remember when they were their children's age and ask them:

- *What would they have wanted?*

Key Points to Remember When Dealing with Children's Grief

All children grieve when they have a significant loss. They grieve in many different ways because of their age, history of loss, cultural norms and other factors. Often children's grief is complicated due to unresolved losses from their past. Be ready to talk about all the losses the child has felt. Children emotionally react when they have survived a traumatic event.

Emotions occur in children when a child almost suffers a loss of a family member or when a friend suffers a loss of someone is close. For example, if they are in a car accident, and none of the passengers was injured, there is emotional trauma and children will react differently from adults. Many adults do not recognize the signs and symptoms of suffering in children. By identifying, the stress signals that a child exhibits and by being supportive, we can help facilitate the normal recovery process from traumatic loss. Stress accumulates, and if children have experienced multiple severe stressors, it can complicate the grieving process.

The goal of crisis counseling is:

- To assist the sufferer through the normal recovery process
- To identify those children who need a referral to mental health professionals
- Not to provide psychotherapy

Children / Post Crisis Behaviors

Everyone's response to the crisis is unique, and those changes frequently fall into patterns. Children are no different, although their stage of development limits their patterns. The following description of typical post-crisis behavioral patterns may be useful for you in observing your children. Consider them as signs of possible prior trauma, or if you know that trauma has occurred, a normal response to the crisis. Notice that the behavioral pattern in each progressive age group may also include some of the previous responses in a crisis.

Pre-School to Kindergarten

Withdrawal - Children may become unusually quiet and seemingly detached from others. They may act subdued and possibly even become mute with adults or peers and be in a state of denial. Denial may take many forms, including denials of facts and memories of events, avoidance of particular issues or themes, ignoring certain people.

Thematic Play - Frequent participation in re-enactment or ritualistic play following a theme of either the trauma itself or life upsets which are secondary to the trauma (such as family problems or physical changes).

Anxious Attachment - Such behavior includes separation and stranger anxiety. Clinging, whining, not letting go of parents is common behavior. Tantrums are frequently observed during a crisis. Since such behavior often occurs during this stage of development, look for changes in frequency and intensity.

Specific Fears - Some common specific fears can include fear of new situations, strangers, males, confinement, violence or certain objects.

Regression - Under severe stress, children attempt to master the situation by reverting to behavioral patterns.

<u>**School Age Children**</u>
Performance Decline - School and intellectual performance, sports, music lessons and hobbies could all be affected.

Compensatory Behaviors - These behaviors may be attempts to deny, reverse or gain retribution for the traumatic experience through fantasy, play or interactions.

Obsessive Talking - The child may continually speak about the incident. It is part of the process of assimilating the event and will be temporary.

A Discrepancy in Mood - The child may express feelings and mood that seem inappropriate to the situation. This may represent an attempt to avoid the full realization of the event or preoccupation with past events.

Psychosomatic Complaints -Stomachaches and headaches are common symptoms of psychological distress. It could also be bids for extra time and attention or other unmet needs.

Adolescents

Acting out Behaviors - They often act out their distress in ways which are ultimately self-destructive. These can include isolation, truancy, drugs and alcohol abuse, hypersexual activity, violence, delinquency, running away, talking about suicide or suicide attempts.

Low Self-esteem and Self-criticism - They may blame themselves and condemn their reactions to crises. They often have fanciful expectations regarding their control over the situation and anything going wrong is a blow to their sense of power and independence.

Displaced Anger - Unable deal with loss and unequipped to control their emotions, you may be the recipient of anger and outburst that has no other place to go.

Preoccupation with Self - Trauma and the resulting inner processing that must take place to sort through the meaning of the incident can intensify the adolescent's normal self-centered preoccupation.

Ways Parents Can Help Their Children

Talk with your children and be honest. Provide simple answers to their questions. If you do not know the answer to a specific question, be honest with the child.

Express your feelings - Let them know that it is acceptable to feel sadness, anger or confusion, etc. Help them understand that these feelings are natural in grieving and are not good or bad. Talk openly about good or bad memories.

LISTEN to what your children say and how they say it. Repeating your children's words and recognizing fear, anxiety, and insecurity is very helpful in helping both you and the children clarify feelings.

OBSERVE your children at play. Pay special attention to what your children say when they play. Frequently children express feelings of fear or anger more openly while playing with their dolls, action figures, or imaginary friends.

REASSURE your children that you will be there for them and you will take care of them. Reassure them that they will be safe and not be abandoned.

ALLOW your children to mourn and grieve in their way and time.

PROVIDE for your children.

Your constant physical presence - Spend extra time putting your child to bed. Leave a night light on if necessary. Hold your child. Touch is important in giving comfort to children during this period.

Remedies for stress symptoms - Teach your children that their physical symptoms i.e. insomnia and headaches are normal when grieving.

Student Notes

_____

_____

_____

_____

_____

_____

_____

_____

_____

_____

_____

_____

_____

_____

_____

_____

_____

_____

_____

_____

_____

_____

_____

_____

LESSON 15

Grief and Bereavement

**Joan Didion wrote in her book,
"*The Year of Magical Thinking*"**
"*Life changes fast, life changes in the instant.*

Immediate response to the death of a loved one is the feeling of shock, numbness and a sense of disbelief. The sufferers may appear as though they are holding up well in front of others. Often, the reality of death has not yet penetrated their awareness. The survivors can seem to be quite accepting of the loss. People feel sadness, loneliness, abandoned regret for a period. Sometimes it is hard to share or even acknowledge the event. The death of loved ones, despite our preparation and age of the person, can deeply traumatize the person and cause emotional triggers. Old memories and feelings that had been long buried and forgotten can resurface and create additional pain.

Grief comes in waves, and there may be moments when the person feels sudden anxiety and the inability to perform daily routines. Extensive research and study have revealed that the power of grief can shock the mind. During the mourning process, the subject may go through a modified and transitory manic-depressive state and often has difficulty dealing with the event. They can be incapable of reasoning (thinking as a child) as if our thoughts or wishing had the power to reverse the narrative, change the outcome of the event. Normal bereavement (uncomplicated grief) usually manifests in temporary anxiety symptoms of insomnia, restlessness, and autonomic nervous system hyperactivity. Pathological grief usually is often associated with a relationship that is dependent on one central figure such as spouse or friend.

A person can become obsessed with the death scene as if rerunning it could somehow reveal a different ending. This behavior can prevent this person from moving forward to normalize their lives. They need to keep the individual who has died alive. Often the despondent refuse to accept the reality of death. Persons feeling of emotional pain are not only upset mentally but are also unbalanced physically. No matter how calm or controlled they a person may seem to be, no person experiencing grief should be expected to act normal at all times.

Definitions, a quick checklist

Grief – is the normal emotional response to a crisis where there has been personal loss. It is unique to the individual who is experiencing the loss and there is no timetable for completing grieving process.

Mourning – The expression of grief and is usually public and common during visitation of the deceased and during the funeral.

Bereavement – describes the event of the loss. The term Bereavement is derived from the Old English word *"berafian" meaning, "to rob".*

Shadow grief – The weeks prior to and after the anniversary of a loved one's death, some bereaved persons experience lethargy, depression and anger similar to their first grief.

Anticipatory grief – occurs prior to death. It is often referred to as "preparatory grief." One can observe the same dynamics as seen in grief after death.

Grief Reactions

Grief is not an illness that needs to be cured. Although grief is a normal response to loss, it sometimes produces unusual and extreme behaviors, which can be frightening to the person experiencing them and of concern to those around them. All of us suffer loss daily in our lives; we are constantly rehearsing the letting go of things, and adjusting to what replaces them. The cycle of loss and renewal is a central concept in human life. Each person will grieve in his or her way. The following descriptions may fit your counselee's reactions.

We should reassure the counselees that it is normal behavior typical of grief. Not all behaviors mentioned are healthy. Some may need to be modified, but they are understandable and do not indicate a pathology that needs to be treated medically.

Acute Reactions

1. Feeling of numbness
2. Reluctance to meet new people Fearful of being alone
3. Afraid to leave the house or fearful of staying in the house
4. Afraid to go to sleep

Physical reactions include

- Tightness in the throat
- Lack of motivation
- Lack of energy to complete common tasks or to finish projects

Some people are more susceptible to colds, flu, and other physical ailments such as skin irritation, an empty feeling in the stomach, and changes in eating habits with significant weight gain or weight loss.

Some people will experience feelings of guilt that somehow they are responsible for the death or not recognizing the warning signs in time to save their loved one.

People often express anger and coldness toward others, especially to family and friends who are trying to give support and sympathy.

> *Survivors will often blame medical personnel for not doing enough or not be successful in saving their loved one.*

Other noticeable reactions

- ✓ Angry that no one seems to understand what the person is going through

- ✓ Angry that people expecting the survivor to "get on with life"
- ✓ Wanting to punish someone or damage something for the pain suffering
- ✓ Feelings of Irritability over small things
- ✓ Unpredictable and uncontrollable weeping
- ✓ Unable to find consolation in faith Inability to carry on a normal conversation
- ✓ Unable to sleep without medication or sleeping all the time
- ✓ Unable to make decisions or to solve common problems
- ✓ Unable to concentrate or remember things Impaired judgment Experience panic attacks
- ✓ Wanting to talk about the deceased but fearful of rejection
- ✓ Wearing clothing, jewelry, or other personal items of the deceased
- ✓ Taking on a lot of the deceased's behavior
- ✓ Feel unbearable loneliness Increase in the use of alcohol and/or prescription drugs to ease the pain.
- ✓ Driving too fast or other reckless behaviors
- ✓ Screaming for no apparent reason

Chronic Reactions

- ✓ Loss of hopes and dreams
- ✓ New events trigger old losses
- ✓ Recurring grief during holidays, anniversaries and birthdays
- ✓ Reluctance to start new relationships

How long grief lasts may sometimes depend on the manner of death, as well as any unresolved issued the person had with the deceased. Going through grief is like taking a journey into unfamiliar territory and is a frightening experience. Navigating through the Grief process can give can give the person a new outlook on life. As counselors, we must encourage people to live in the moment and embrace the people in their lives, by doing so life will become more meaningful.

When to Make a Referral

Every so often, a counselee may come to us with an issue that requires immediate attention or a prompt referral to a healthcare professional (e.g., a psychiatrist, psychologist, or medical doctor).

The following are some of the crises that counselors may need to refer

Grief and Bereavement

There may a need for additional training for this specific type of counseling.

Severe Clinical Depression

Verbalized threat of suicide needs emergency intervention from healthcare professionals; may require "911" intervention. Never ignore a person who threatens to kill himself.

Mental Breakdown

Mental breakdowns may exceed the experience of the spiritual counselor and may require a referral to healthcare professionals.

Bizarre Behavior

Bizarre Behavior may be a sign of mental illness may require immediate medical and psychological attention. Counselors should not assign a psychological diagnosis to the counselee (e.g., psychosis, schizophrenia), unless we are trained psychology professionals.

Our Goal in Helping People

Our goals as counselors are simple, and they help to create a framework within which Biblical counseling can operate. Seeing problems from a Biblical perspective helps us understand how God views these issues. Seeing things through God's eyes helps us choose to accept His way for resolving problems.

Student Notes

_____

_____

_____

_____

_____

_____

_____

_____

_____

_____

_____

_____

_____

_____

_____

_____

_____

_____

_____

_____

_____

_____

_____

_____

_____

_____

_____

LESSON 16

Healing Conversations

Now equipped with the understanding of the grieving process and the symptoms that can result from personal loss, the counselor is better able to comfort to the sufferer using healing conversations.

There are four (4) steps to the conversation process.

Step 1 – FACTS – a non-intrusive inquiry into specifics

"Where were you when _____?"

"How did you hear about _____?"

Step 2 – THOUGHTS – encourage linking of facts

"What did you think when _____?"

What was going through your mind when ____?

"When you look back, what do you think about _____?"

"Describe any disturbing thoughts about ____?"

Step 3 – FEELINGS/REACTIONS – support and encourage

"I can hear how much you miss_____"

"What touched you the most about__?"

"You seem pretty shaken by _____"

Step 4 – REASSURANCE – normalization and education

"It is okay to cry"

"I am sorry you are having such a difficult time"

"One resource you may want to tap into is _____"

Counselors should remember the following points when counseling the bereaved

1. Confidentiality
2. Use conversational tone
3. The steps above should flow naturally as we are conversing
4. Being present demonstrates you care and want to help.
5. Use good active listening skills.
6. Avoid criticism

7. Humor can be an useful assessment tool

8. Don't lose our cool – get comfortable with anger

9. Problem resolution should not be pushy

10. Allow the bereaved to vent before we provide information or teaching

11. If this conversation is being done on the telephone:

12. Avoid call waiting and other distractions

13. Keep background noise to a minimum

14. Use minimal encouragers to make sure they know you are there and listening

15. Some people will open up more on the phone than in person

16. (There is safety in anonymity) but more difficult for counselors without halo data.

Communicating with those in Grief

In a simple and direct way, express our sorrow about the counselee's loss. Mention the deceased by name or the specific sad event. Do not encourage the griever to get rid of the deceased belongings. Share your happy memories, the more specific, the more meaningful:

- Advice they gave us
- Something they said or did that touched us
- Virtues, achievements, successes for which they'll be remembered

- Do not be afraid to express your own sense of loss
- Do not worry about making the griever cry

We did not put the tears there and we cannot take them away. Crying together is better than trying to avoid the pain

DO SAY:

- "It is a great sorrow for us all"
- "I feel fortunate to have known…."
- "I feel the loss of ……"
- "I am greatly saddened by …."
- "Please accept my/our sincere condolences/sympathy"
- "My heart / prayers /thoughts /sympathies are with you and your family"
- "He or she will be long remembered for."
- "I feel privileged to have counted (name) as a friend"
- "While no words of mine can ease your loss, I just wanted you to know that I am grieving with you and your family"

Be careful of Clichés

Anyone who has received the condolences from others has encountered some of the well-meaning but hurtful **clichés, false cheerfulness and optimistic platitudes** that pass for expressions of sympathy. Counselors should keep in mind the following guidelines in what not to say or ask, so we can avoid burdening the bereaved with unhelpful verbiage.

Avoid excessive dramatic language ("dreadful, horrible, appalling news" etc." Avoid pious clichés, simplistic explanations, or presumptive interpretations of God's intents or involvement in this sorrowful event.

Do not give advice Avoid generic offers of help. Be specific

NEVER SAY:

- "I know just how you feel"
- "Be happy for what you have"
- "Are you over it yet?"
- "Don't cry"
- "Life is for the living"
- "He/she was too young to die"
- "At least you had him/her for twenty years"

- "I feel almost worse than you do"
- "God had a purpose in sending you this burden, you are stronger now"

NO NEED TO REASSURE

- "At least his/her suffering is over"
- "He/she is in a better place now"
- "You'll feel better soon. It takes time, that's all"
- "Be brave"
- "Life must go on. Time heals all wounds. You'll feel better before you know it"
- "Thank God you have other children"

Student Notes

LESSON 17

Preparing for Approaching Death

When a person enters the final stage of the dying process, two different dynamics are at work. Physically, the body begins the orderly progressive series of physical changes in the final process of shutting down. These physical changes are a normal way in which the body prepares itself to stop. The most appropriate interventions should be focused on comfort enhancing for the dying. Other dynamics of the dying process is on the emotional, spiritual and mental aspects.

The "spirit" of the dying person begins the final process of release from the body, its immediate environment, and all attachments. This release may depend on resolving unfinished issues and receiving permission to "let go" from family members. These "events" are natural in the spiritual preparation to move from this existence to the next dimension. The most appropriate responses to these changes are those, which support and encourage this release and peaceful transition.

If they die today, are they ready to meet Jesus?

When a person is not spiritually ready and has unresolved issues, or perhaps they have yet to reconcile certain relationships, he or she may tend to linger to finish the task. The process of dying happens in a way that is unique and appropriate for the values, beliefs, and lifestyle of the dying person. Therefore, as you seek to prepare yourself as the event approaches, you may want to know what to expect and how to respond in ways that will help your loved one accomplish this transition with support, understanding, and ease.

Normal Physiological Signs and Symptoms for the Final Stages of Life

Bedside manners - In hospital, situations do not talk about the person in their presence. Speak to them directly and normally even though there may be no response. Never assume the person cannot hear because hearing is the last of the senses to be lost. The person may seem confused about the time, place and identity of people surrounding them. Identify yourself by name before speaking rather than ask the person to guess who you are.

Giving Permission – Giving permission for your loved one to let go without making them feel guilty for leaving or trying to keep them with you to meet your own needs can be difficult. A dying person will normally try to hold on, even though it brings prolonged discomfort, in order to be sure that those who are going to be left behind will be all right. Therefore, your ability to release the dying person from this concern and give them assurance that is alright to let go whenever they are ready is one of the greatest gift for your loved one at this time.

Saying Good-Bye– When a person is ready to die and you are able to let go, then it is time to say "good-bye". This is your final gift of love to them for it achieves closure and makes the final release possible. It may be helpful to lay in bed with the person and hold them or to take their hand and say everything you need to say. **It may be as simple as "I love you". It may include recounting favorite memories, places, and activities you shared. It may include saying, "I'm sorry for whatever I contributed to any tensions or difficulties in our relationship"**. It may also include saying "thank you for…"

Things to Know About the Dying

1. What are their fears?

2. What are their hopes and expectations?

3. What is their unfinished business?

Some of the Fears the Dying May Face

1. Loss of control

2. Loss of personal identity

3. Ceasing to be

4. The unknown

5. What happens after death

6. Loss of relationship

7. Incompleteness or lack of meaning in their lives

8. Being a burden

9. Loneliness

10. The dying process itself

    a. Will it be painful

    b. How long will it take?

    c. Will I be abandoned?

    d. Will I lose my dignity?

Some of the Hopes and Decries of the Dying

1. Getting well and be productive again

2. Die with dignity and be surrounded by caring people

3. To be able to maintain some degree of control

4. To be able to express their needs and feelings openly

5. To be able to manage their pain

Some of Their Unfinished Business

1. Seeing a significant person who is far away
2. Taking one more trip to a special place
3. Completing an unfinished project
4. Providing for loved ones
5. Healing any estrangements; feeling forgiven

Habits of Effective Comforters

Decreased Socialization– The person may want to be with one or only a few people. This is a sign of preparation for release and an affirming of which the support is most needed from to make the appropriate transition. If you are not a part of this inner circle at the end, it does not mean you are not loved or are unimportant. It means you have already fulfilled your task with him/her and it is the time for you to say "good-bye". If you are a part of the final inner circle of support, the person needs your affirmation, support, and permission.

Giving Permission– Giving permission for your loved one to let go without making them feel guilty for leaving or trying to keep them with you to meet your own needs can be difficult. **A dying person will normally try to hold on,** even though it brings prolonged discomfort, to be sure that those who are going to be left behind will be all right. Therefore, your ability to release the dying person from this concern and give them assurance that is alright to let go whenever they are ready is one of the greatest gifts for your loved one at this time.

Saying Good-Bye– When a person is ready to die, and you can let go, then it is time to say "good-bye". This is your final gift of love to them for it achieves closure and makes the final release possible. It may be helpful to lay in bed with the person and hold them or to take their hand and say everything you need to say. It may be as simple as "I love you". It may include recounting favorite memories, places, and activities you shared. It may include saying, "I'm sorry for whatever I contributed to any tensions or difficulties in our relationship". It may also include saying "thank you for..." Tears do not be afraid to cry with the person. Tears express your love and help you to let go. [xiv]

Student Notes

LESSON 18

Chaplain and Volunteers Serving in the Prisons

. . . I was in prison, and you came to me.
(Matthew 25:36)

When arrested, law enforcement will book the arrestee into custody at the county receiving facility where the jailer, detention officer or deputy will take charge of the prisoner and continue the intake process. If any prisoner is combative, suicidal, or is a crucial witness to a crime, prisoners will be placed in segregated housing for their safety or the safety of others. Eventually, inmates are placed in a pretrial facility while awaiting a trial or final sentencing. The charges that land people in jail or prison are vast in number and may be a simple as non-violent crimes such as check and credit card fraud to first-degree murder.

The most common arrest is usually drug related and involves criminal activities such as drug use, trafficking, distribution, and burglary. Predatory crimes such as child molestation, rape, and murder are part of the plethora of crimes that a chaplain must contend with from both a religious and security standpoint.

The newly incarcerated are sometimes in denial of their circumstance resulting in combative behavior by the inmate or in the case the inmate who is arrested for driving while under the influence (DUI) will be too intoxicated to have a reasonable conversation. It is essential to be mindful of the security and informational risk when ministering to an inmate. If the inmate is involved in a case that is sensitive, the chaplain must maintain absolute confidence in the matter so as not to impair evidence or witness testimony that may eventually be introduced at trial. In most cases, the inmate will be transferred to a Pre-Trial facility while awaiting trial unless there is a specific mandate that prohibits the inmate from transfer to a facility where the inmate may come into contact with a potential witness or possible victim (a Keep-away).

In the County Jail inmate housing will differ depending on the security level of the inmate and can range from minimum security to maximum-security degrees. Some county jails classify their inmates by using a color-coded wristband system that will immediately identify the inmate's security level and risk. In some facilities, an inmate wearing a blue band may indicate that the individual is a sexual predator or child molester while an orange band may designate the person as a danger to staff. Violent individuals will typically remain in handcuffs at all times during cell movement.

Maximum Security Inmates

Access to maximum-security inmates often comes with restrictions due to safety issues. In the State and Federal prison system, security classification of inmates will determine the level of the institution where an inmate will do his or her time of incarceration. By understanding, the duties of a chaplain and the surrounding environment will provide an atmosphere of safety and success.

Comparative Duties

FULL TIME CHAPLAIN DUTIES AND RESPONSIBILITY	VOLUNTEER CHAPLAIN DUTIES AND RESPONSIBILITY
Administrative • Correctional staff • Security staff • Associate Wardens • Warden • Training Department • Government audits **Religious services** • Provide religious programing • Coordinating religious groups • Baptisms • Counseling • Death Notifications • Crisis Intervention and more	**Volunteerism** • Providing religious services • Counseling • Special Programs • Baptisms

If you are serving as a paid chaplain for the Federal Bureau of Prisons (BOP), the scope of chaplaincy will far exceed that of your religious persuasion. While a BOP chaplain is required to perform the ordinances of their faith to the incarcerated of similar background, the chaplain will be asked to manage the needs of other religious groups. The chaplain is not required to perform services for those are in different communities of belief. However, the chaplain will be needed to address the issues of religious diets, religious holidays, and religious supplies, perform death notifications as well as be available to meet the counseling need of the inmate population both religious and non-religious.

Institutional chaplains also are burdened with the duties of overseeing religious volunteers, volunteer training, maintaining chapel records, having a working knowledge of the government database and preparing the Religious Services Department for government audits. State facilities often assign their chaplains duties within their faith group through their required duties and mandates may be similar to that of a federal chaplain.

Volunteer chaplains have fewer restrictions and are primarily concerned with meeting the personal religious needs of the inmate as prescribed by their system of beliefs. If a county, detention facility or local jail does not have an on-duty chaplain available during a time of crisis, the volunteer chaplain may be asked to provide emergency services such as death notifications and crisis (Spiritual) counseling. In general, the volunteer chaplain (Religious volunteer) will conduct religious services and work under the authority of the chaplain or volunteer coordinator.

Whether you are a full time or volunteer chaplain, you will be required to receive four to six hours of orientation training before officiating religious services to the inmate population for the first time. Orientation will include instruction on the Prison Rape Elimination Act (PREA), entrance and exit procedures, inmate manipulation and con games, hostage situations, security protocols and more. Volunteerism should never minimize institutional safety and security. As a volunteer, you will be exposed to institutional operations and will be expected to maintain the same level of security as any security or correctional staff member. Any concerns should be addressed to the on-duty chaplain or volunteer coordinator.

Prison Rape Elimination Act

During the George Bush presidency, the Prison Rape Elimination Act (PREA) was established to reduce the number inmate rape in the jail and prison system in the United States and unanimously passed by both houses of government. While many institutions are playing catchup establishing PREA protocols, most prison facilities have PREA protocols in place, require both staffs, and volunteer to be familiar with inmate victimization. More than likely during the orientation process staff and volunteers will receive instruction on the topic. As a chaplain or volunteer, the rules that regulate mandated reporting applies and if an inmate approaches you regarding a violation, confidentiality cannot be offered.

Definition of Sexual Misconduct

Any behavior or act of a sexual nature, directed toward a person under the care, custody, or the supervision of the custodial institution regardless if the participants claim that the encounter is consensual.

Statistics

65% male, 35% female

47% between the ages of 18 & 25

53% White

35% Black, non-Hispanic

11% Hispanic

January 2011, Bureau of Justice Statistics

Victims who suffer from sexual abuse are:

- 3 times more likely to suffer from depression
- 4 times more likely to commit suicide
- 6 times more likely to suffer from PTSD
- 13 times more likely to abuse alcohol
- 26 times more likely to abuse drugs

Only 5-10% of reports of sexual abuse are reported by staff members 27% of reports are reported by their family members

The reason for PREA

In 2003, the U.S. Congress passed the Prison Rape Elimination Act. The act required the establishment of the National Prison Rape Elimination Commission to:

- Develop national standards for the prevention of Sexual Misconduct including a zero-tolerance policy.
- Make data on prison rape available to administrators.

- Make correctional agencies more accountable for Sexual Misconduct in their facilities.
- Conduct studies regarding the impact of the adoption of a zero-tolerance policy affected agencies.
- This act was passed unanimously by all 583 members of Congress.

There is NO Such Thing as Sexual Consent between Staff or Inmates

Any sexual activities whether perpetrated by staff or inmate is punishable by imprisonment

Failure to Act Could Lead To Criminal Prosecution or Civil Damages

It is the responsibility of all staff to take immediate action when sexual assaults are reported. Zero (0%) Tolerance for Sexual Abuse & Sexual Harassment Sexual misconduct, sexual harassment and sexual assault is an abuse of power on the part of the correctional staff and is unacceptable. All prisons and county jails have a "ZERO TOLERANCE" standard for such acts of sexual abuse against persons in its care and custody.

Mandatory Reporting Laws - Per PREA Standard 115.61

Staff and agency reporting duties

The prison system requires all staff and volunteers to report any, suspicion, or information regarding an incident of sexual abuse or sexual harassment that occurred in a facility.

Response Protocol

It is not necessary to make a judgment about whether or not a sexual assault occurred. Separate the victim and if known, the abuser. Preserve and protect any crime scene until the collection of evidence. Request that the victim does not take any actions that could destroy evidence. The following is the initial response protocol that should happen when a PREA incident has occurred.

Activate alarm if needed

- Take the alleged victim to a private, secure location, bag hands. (Paper Bag)
- Contact Supervisor/inform
- Separate victim/suspect
- Secure crime scene
- Listen to victim, take notes
- Assess medical and custody needs
- Initiate time log (Inmate Victim PREA)
- Give time log to supervisor upon arrival.

Preservation of Evidence

At all times during this procedure, it is imperative to make effort to ensure that both the victim and suspect DO NOT:

- Shower
- Wash Hands
- Brush Teeth Or Rinse Mouth
- Remove Clothing Without Medical Supervision
- Use Restroom Facilities
- Consume Any Liquids

Victims & Perpetrators

The Victim

- First-time, non-violent inmates
- Detained on a sexual offense against a minor
- Physically small or weak
- Traits viewed as effeminate
- Not streetwise
- Mental illness
- Disliked by other inmates/staff

The Perpetrator

- Accustomed to prison
- Previous incarceration
- Gang affiliated
- Committed a violent offense

- Physically strong
- Likely to break prison rules

Dynamics of Sexual Abuse / Harassment in Confinement

The main dynamics, as experienced by inmates, are Power, Dominance and Control.

Common Reactions of Victims of Sexual Abuse / Harassment

Common reactions to sexual assault are broken down into three categories:

- **Emotional responses**
- **cognitive responses (knowledge or awareness)**
- **Behavioral responses**

Communicating With the Victim

- Be sincere without appearing to make accusations, lay blame, or make accusations particularly when dealing with lesbian, gay, bisexual, transgender, intersex or gender non-conforming offenders (LGBT).
- Allow offender to talk while you actively listen.
- Be sure to show verbal and non-verbal signs of interest in the discussion.

- Assure confidentiality, but be clear that rule infractions, security issues, and relevant information must be reported per policy.

Treat all inmates in a humane manner and with respect for the inherent dignity of the human person.

Student Notes

_____

_____

_____

_____

_____

_____

_____

_____

_____

_____

_____

_____

_____

_____

_____

_____

_____

_____

_____

_____

_____

_____

_____

_____

_____

BONUS LESSON 19

CHAPLAIN VOLUNTEERS SERVING IN THE PRISONS

ANATOMY OF A SETUP

Since inmate manipulation of staff is an urgent problem in the prison system, the chaplain and chaplain volunteer must be aware of their surroundings and be cautious of overly friendly inmate behavior. Some inmates may try to find some common ground with a staff member to establish a relationship, thus creating a portal for staff abuse. While the religious community enjoys more liberties than most correctional staff when it comes to inmate contact, care should be taken, and the chaplain and volunteer should always maintain a professional relationship with the inmate population at all times to avoid the danger of inmate manipulation. The following is a set of guidelines that will help correctional workers determine if a staff member has been compromised.

The Model Inmate

Inmates can be like predators and chameleons, changing their demeanor, mood, and behavior to get their prey. The model inmate is a skilled actor. Not all inmates fall in to the category of manipulator and most are grateful for the care that is provided by the religious services department however, there are those inmates who are willing to cross boundaries in order to accomplish their goal.

How to Prevent Boundary Violations

- Avoid identifying with inmates.
- Never place yourself in a situation where a sense of obligation exists.
- Use empathy instead of sympathy with inmates.

How to Prevent Boundary Violations

If you strictly adhere to the following principles would-be manipulators will leave you alone. In fact, most inmates will look to you as someone they can trust and emulate.

1. Never do anything to, for, or with an inmate that you would be ashamed to share with your peers or supervisor.
2. Keep everything out in the open.

Guidelines for Self-Evaluation

- Am I overly friendly or familiar?
- Do I appear gullible?
- Do inmates consider me too trusting?
- Am I sympathetic?
- Is my demeanor timid?
- Is my enforcement of rules non-existent, or consistent?
- Do I share personal problems with inmates?
- Do I check the validity of inmate information?
- Do I let things slide, which should be addressed immediately?
- Do I have difficulty with command, control, or saying no?
- Do I circumvent minor rules?
- Do I allow the taking of liberties?
- Can I be made to feel obligated?
- Am I easily distracted?

Continued Guidelines for Self-Evaluation

Recognizing one is vulnerable does not mean one is unfit for a career in corrections. Neither does it mean you must change your personality. It does mean you need an alternative approach to your way of dealing with inmates. Stop the game before it begins.

- Most volunteers violate boundaries out of naiveté or ignorance.
- Most withdraw from the game because of a distinct feeling that "something is not quite right."

For whatever reason, we realize what is going on before it is too late.

Contributing Factors

- Isolated posts, jobs, areas
- Learn the job from an inmate
- Staff have to "pay their dues"
- We did it and succeeded, so should they!

Awareness

- Friendliness and Over-Familiarization
- Appearance and Body Language
- Listening Observation
- Selection of a Victim – Intentional and Accidental
- Testing Staff/Rule Bending/Asking for Things
- Support System/We – They Syndrome
- Plea for Help
- Offer of Protection

- Allusions to Sex
- Touch System
- Rumor Mill

Are We Paying Attention to the Inmate?

- Over-identifying with inmates "My Inmate"
- Horse-play with inmates
- Inmate know personal staff information
- Inmates with letters/photos of staff
- Staff granting special requests or favors
- Inmates repeatedly in unauthorized areas
- Staff spending an unexplainable amount of time with inmates

Summary

Length of service, education, or experience has no direct bearing on selection.

New employees are especially vulnerable due to a lack of understanding of their job and environment.
Experienced employees become vulnerable because they become too comfortable with their jobs.

The challenge in corrections is to meet the daily institutional needs and develop your own mental and emotional health.

Remain careful, alert, and aware that some inmates are constantly seeking to victimize or compromise you!

CONGRATULATIONS YOU ARE DONE!

Student Notes

_____

_____

_____

_____

_____

_____

_____

_____

_____

_____

_____

_____

_____

_____

_____

_____

_____

_____

_____

_____

_____

_____

_____

_____

Special Thanks to our Resource Providers

[i] By (CI) Chaplain Norberto Guzman, B.A., M.C.C. / Signet Bible College and Theological Seminary

[ii] By (CI) Chaplain Norberto Guzman, B.A., M.C.C. / Signet Bible College and Theological Seminary

[iii] "Serving Those Who Serve - Glatfelter Insurance Group." Insert Name of Site in Italics. N.p., n.d. Web. 29 Sep. 2016 https://secure.glatfelters.com/vfis/vfisshopcart.nsf/(Web+Downloads+by+Category)

[iv] Naomi K. Paget. *The Work of the Chaplain*. Judson press 2006. Valley Forge, PA.

[v]http://study.com/articles/Hospital_Chaplain

[vi] Hospice Chaplain Duties - Chaplain Job Description. (n.d.). Retrieved from http://www.change-career-with-purpose.com/hospicechaplainduties.html

[vii]T5360.02 Ministry of a BOP Chaplain / Technical Reference Manual

[viii] The Journal of the American Academy of Psychiatry / The Law in the case of Lightman v. Flaum, 687 N.Y.S.2d 562 (N.Y. Sup. Ct. 1999)
[ix]
enrichmentjournal.ag.org/201002/ejonline_201002_Pastor_Confid_.cfm

[x] Signet Bible College and Theological Seminary /Ethics course curriculum

[xi] National Sheriffs Association – Chaplains Reference Guide

[xii] National Sheriffs Association – Chaplains Reference Guide

[xiii]Adam Pulaski, Steve Lihn / Biblical Counseling Manual (2004) / 2.1. Diagnosis

[xiv] .legacy-hospice.com." Insert Name of Site in Italics. N.p., n.d. Web. 29 Sep. 2016 <http://www.legacy-

hospice.com/media/Patients%20&%20Families/Caregiver's%20Gu>.

"preparing for the dying process - floyd.org." Insert Name of Site in Italics. N.p., n.d. Web. 29 Sep. 2016 <https://www.floyd.org/services/Documents/palliative-care-resources-802-816-prepa>.

CHAPLAINCY 101

Preparing For Approaching Death - Hospice,
https://hospicenet.org/html/preparing_for.html (accessed September 29, 2016).

Dr. Paul Mikus, Th.D., Signet Bible College and Theological Seminary
Edward Ehee, B.A. Signet Bible College and Theological Seminary
Dr. Vu Le, M.D., Signet Bible College and Theological Seminary

Dr. Jay Adams

.

CPSIA information can be obtained
at www.ICGtesting.com
Printed in the USA
LVHW021557200219
608187LV00033B/871/P

9 781542 754675